D0875209

LOUIS SULLIVAN

THE MASTERS OF
WORLD ARCHITECTURE SERIES

UNDER THE GENERAL EDITORSHIP OF WILLIAM ALEX

ALVAR AALTO by Frederick Gutheim
LE CORBUSIER by Françoise Choay
ANTONIO GAUDÍ by George R. Collins
WALTER GROPIUS by James M. Fitch
ERIC MENDELSOHN by Wolf Von Eckardt
LUDWIG MIES VAN DER ROHE by Arthur Drexler
PIER LUIGI NERVI by Ada Louise Huxtable
RICHARD NEUTRA by Esther McCoy
OSCAR NIEMEYER by Stamo Papadaki
LOUIS SULLIVAN by Albert Bush-Brown
FRANK LLOYD WRIGHT by Vincent Scully, Jr.

louis sullivan

by Albert Bush-Brown

George Braziller, Inc.
NEW YORK, 1960

For information address the publisher,
George Braziller, Inc.,
215 Park Avenue South,
New York 3, N.Y.

Library of Congress Catalog Card Number: 60-13306

Printed in the United States of America

ACKNOWLEDGMENT

An interpretive essay that surrounds an artist with the philosophical currents of his own time and assesses his legacy necessarily relies upon the scholarship of many authors. The meaning of Louis Sullivan's idea has been clarified and nobly broadcast by Hugh Morrison, Henry-Russell Hitchcock, Grant Manson, Lewis Mumford, Donald Drew Egbert, Edgar Kaufmann, Jr., and Henry R. Hope, whose contributions to this essay are gratefully recorded in the bibliography.

A. B.-B.

CONTENTS

. . . The architect who combines in his being the powers of vision, of imagination, of intellect, of sympathy with human need and the power to interpret them in a language vernacular and true—is he who shall create poems in stone . . .

LOUIS H. SULLIVAN

"Concerning the Imperial Hotel, Tokyo, Japan"
Architectural Record, April, 1923, p. 333

ONLY THE HEROIC SCALE measures Louis Sullivan. The titanic task he set himself was to shape his society through architecture, as the Parthenon did for Athens, the Cathedral for Paris. He was the first prophet to build for the American condition. His childhood dream, the mighty Craftsman, was a grandiose vision come to a boy on a farm during a summer vacation, but it had the drive and momentum of a whole civilization.

At eighteen, standing in the Sistine Chapel, he communed in silence with "The first mighty man of Courage . . . power as he had seen it in the mountains, . . . in the open sky, . . . the primal power of Life at work." He saw imagination there, imagination speaking truths beyond reason, timelessly, mysteriously revealing "uncompromising faith in Life, as faith in man. . . . "[1]

He determined to seek the forces at work in his own society, to organize them, lead them toward humane ends, and express them in the plastic, rhythmic fluency of buildings. That his vision excelled his accomplishment was a hero's fate; that his prophecy went largely unheeded and unrewarded gave tragic scope, not to himself, but to his purpose, as he intimated by telling his life-story in the third person and calling it, *The Autobiography of an Idea.*

To explain that idea, Louis Sullivan ever sought an image. Words, however lyric (and he commanded many), had no power to gain a "ten-fingered grasp" of what the American landscape might hold;[2] buildings, however closely they captured his spirit, froze the idea, failed to suggest a dynamic architecture. For the American architecture should be born new each day, spring fresh from its soil, its period, its civilization, modified by an environment which, itself, changed continuously as the American political epic unfolded.

1. *AN ELM IN FOUR SEASONS*

TRYING IN HIS last and disappointed years to suggest that idea, Sullivan returned to metaphor, to an elm tree he had seen as a child on his grandfather's farm. Solitary in the meadow, it presented " . . . such tall slender grace [as] he had never seen. Its broad slim fronds spreading so high and descending in lovely curves . . . , he became infiltrated, suffused, inspired with the fateful sense of beauty."[3]

Here was no inspiration derived from the temples and cathedrals of a past society, no pawing over books illustrating historic architecture; while others might vainly copy Mont St. Michel line for line, while still others might seek sources in geometry, as Palladio had, or in machinery, as engineers did, Sullivan turned to living forms. His primal source was the organism, for it offered the basic law governing growth, a law that related the shape of a thing to its innermost nature and to its way of adapting itself to its environment: " . . . the function of a building must . . . organize its form."[4]

That was an epochal statement, the germ of the first new architectural theory since the eighteenth century's conflicting philosophies of romanticism and mechanism. At a single stroke, Sullivan's law cut through both earlier theories; it provided a mechanical basis for structure and function, and romantic expression besides: " . . . as, for instance, the oak tree expressed the function oak, the pine tree the function pine."[5]

While the metaphor and the law had been hinted at by earlier philosophers, as will be discussed later, Sullivan showed how the theory could be built in brick and steel that were carried on caissons sunk deep in the earth of the American city. There stands at Buffalo, for example, the noble Guaranty Building (plates 54–64), later called the Prudential, built in 1894–95 when Sullivan stood at the summit of his practice. A giant in scale, if not in size, it stands among masonry and steel-borne buildings, many of which tower above it, but it alone is memorable because it alone allowed its purpose to organize its mass, to suggest how steel and bronze and terra cotta might cease being inert and spring into life.

The Guaranty, like every other problem in architectural design, suggested its own solution: at least, that was Sullivan's thesis in an article he wrote for *Lippincott's Magazine* in 1896. What are the practical functions to be met? *First,* a story below ground containing the boilers whose heat will warm the building, whose power will run its lights, pumps and elevators; *second,* a ground floor devoted to stores, banks and establishments that require ready access, ample light, and large areas; *third,* a second story, accessible by stairways, with liberal structural spacing and wide expanses of glass; *fourth,* above the two-story base, an indefinite range of offices piled tier on tier, each office like all others, cells in a honeycomb; *fifth,* the summit, a large attic where the tanks, valves, pipes and sheaves mutely witness the elevator cables making their "grand turn, ascending and descending."[6]

"Hence," wrote Sullivan, as though he had suddenly arrived at the major thrust of a geometric proof, "it follows inevitably, and in the simplest possible way, that . . . we will in the following manner design the exterior of our tall office building —to wit:"[7] Starting with the first story, we shall meet an attractive gateway, the entrance, which will stand among large rooms, to be treated expansively, based on their practical necessities, but also sumptuously, befitting their use; and the second story, though less pretentious, will receive similar treatment. Above this, the standard office room will determine the standard structural unit, an individual cell with a window framed by its piers, sill and lintel, and the units will "look all alike because they all are alike."[8] Then, eventually, we shall arrive at the attic where, with one broad flourish, we may forcefully terminate the whole expanse of wall.

As yet, we have only a bald result—logical and coherent enough, organized in accordance with the factual purposes of spaces and their structural supports—but "we must now heed the imperative voice of emotion."[9]

What is the signal feature of the tall office building? "And at once we answer, it is lofty. This loftiness is . . . its thrilling aspect. It is the very open organ-tone in its appeal. . . . It must be tall. . . . It must be every inch a proud and soaring thing, rising in sheer exultation that from bottom to top it is a unit without a single dissenting line. . . . "[10] Accordingly, to express his emotional grasp of the practical conditions, Sullivan boldly tossed the Guaranty's vertical piers skyward; each one rapidly ascends, indeed, soars past the meadow of rich ornament on the window spandrels, until it bursts its slender grace and spreads swirls and tufts of leaves across the skyline.

For anyone who has ever seen it, except regrettably for the men of Buffalo who have progressively defaced it, the Guaranty Building is the consummate statement of America's first urge to give appropriate, beautiful shape to the environment of industrial society. It resolved the plaguing schism in nineteenth-century attitudes, where the raw world of science, industrial technique and commercial enterprise stood across the tracks from the world of culture, a world of imagination and spiritual ideals shamelessly cloaked in the Gothic and Classic mantles reserved for churches, museums, and universities.

Sullivan resolved the dualism; he united utility with beauty in the service of a modern institution. His inspiration arrived in a pasture with an elm tree; its realization came at Buffalo, when Louis Sullivan was 39.

2. *SUMMER INSPIRATION*

LOUIS SULLIVAN was born in Boston in 1856, the son of immigrant parents; his Irish father, a fiddler and dancing master, had arrived in 1847, established a dancing academy, and married Andrienne Françoise List, of Swiss-French and German parentage. Somewhat itinerant, the parents sent the five-year-old Louis Sullivan to live with his maternal grandparents on their farm at South Reading, Massachusetts, where he spent most summers until he was fourteen. In 1869, his family moved to Chicago, leaving Louis with his grandparents while he commuted to school in Boston.

His *Autobiography* vividly recalls his early years: his awakening to rhythm as he watched street sweepers move through Boston; to power as he allowed water to burst a dam he had built across a small brook; to craftsmanship as he studied a cobbler at work; to romance as he listened to the Gaelic tales told by Julia, the hired girl on the farm.

Overall, the *Autobiography* tells of his great identification with nature, almost a pantheistic adoration (surely magnified in recall); something more precise, a regard for fact and logic—at his grandfather's side learning about the moon, at English High gaining respect for number and grammar; and, withal, an emotional tone quickened by his mother's skillful playing at the piano.

And there was one awesome scene, when the young Sullivan wandered away from a family picnic, got lost in the woods, and looked down upon a dark, ominous shape: a chain suspension bridge stretched across the Merrimack River; his father rescued the trembling boy and gently turned his nightmare thoughts of sinister giants into a vision of mighty men who built heroically. The image never left him.

Ever nostalgic about the countryside, fettered by the city, Sullivan seems not to have enjoyed Boston, except that buildings there began to speak to him ("Some said vile things, some said prudent things . . . , but none said noble things."[11]), especially one building, the Masonic Temple, and Commonwealth Avenue, where he glimpsed his first architect and admired his cavalier departure in a fine carriage.

SULLIVAN'S EDUCATION

Determined at that instant, so he later said, to become an architect, Sullivan at 16 entered the Massachusetts Institute of Technology where, in 1872, the first American school of architecture had been in operation for seven years. Its director, William Ware, had long followed the English vogue for Gothic, evident in his designs for Memorial Hall at Cambridge and the First Unitarian Church at Boston. Both were modeled upon the Victorian Gothic style practiced by William Butterfield and George Edmund Street in England and championed by the English critic, John Ruskin. But Ware's educational scope exceeded his professional allegiances, and he brought Eugene Létang, a graduate of the Parisian Ecole des Beaux-Arts to teach at M.I.T. Under Létang in the drafting room, Sullivan was introduced to the elements—the "orders": columns, bases, capitals and cornices of classical architectural vocabulary; concerned largely with styles, the instruction struck Sullivan as a mere "misch-masch of architectural theology."[12]

He left M.I.T. at the end of the year and went to New York hoping possibly to gain work with Richard Morris Hunt, the architectural lion there; but Hunt offered only anecdotes of his days at the Ecole in 1845, and Sullivan went south to Philadelphia, where his eye was attracted by a building designed by Frank Furness, whom he visited immediately. Furness, the architect of the Pennsylvania Academy of the Fine Arts (plate 1), hired the young draftsman, only to lose him when the depression of 1873 forced Furness to reduce his staff. Sullivan joined his parents in Chicago; arriving there after the Fire, when all the architectural offices, good and bad, were feverishly rebuilding, he saw the city as " . . . magnificent and wild: A crude extravaganza, An intoxicating rawness. . . . "[13] He entered the employ of William le Baron Jenney, but soon quit and sailed from New York, July 10, 1874, for another try at education, this time in Paris.

At Liverpool for a day or two, then down to London for two weeks, Sullivan probably moved too quickly to study Liverpool's Oriel Chambers (1864) and other examples of articulated iron construction that anticipated American work on commercial buildings. And then in Paris, Sullivan entered a rooming-house in the Latin Quarter, studied for the Ecole's stiff entrance examinations, passed them successfully, and joined the atelier Vaudremer, "the damnedest pig-sty I ever got into."[14]

Again Sullivan was set to work on the "orders." After one exhausting project, he made a trip to Rome and Florence, and, apparently, quit the Ecole. His later work amply indicates that his French education taught him composition, and privately he admitted as much, most notably in his confidence to Claude Bragdon —that the Ecole gave him a firm education in logic[15]—but publicly, especially when a misunderstood version of Beaux-Arts architecture began to dominate the American scene from the nineties onward, Sullivan was critical of the French school. He seems to have preferred not to specify the duration of his stay there; indeed, his *Autobiography* implies that he was abroad about two years; but recent evidence indicates that his sojourn lasted six months, for he was back in Chicago by March, 1875.

ARCHITECTURAL TASTE IN 1875

Judged in its fullest national stature, the architectural scene that greeted Sullivan upon his return in 1875 presented the schizoid duality of a nation that was as yet undecided whether it would stand for something new, or remain a condescending cousin of Imperial Europe, ashamed of its subordinate station and anxious to acquire European culture as rapidly as possible.

The cast-iron stores and warehouses in Baltimore, New York and Boston, or along the River at St. Louis, presaged a new architecture, arisen to house a society bent on industry and commerce; technological institutions—Cornell, M.I.T., R.P.I. —announced an education for engineers; and, in 1876, the Johns Hopkins University opened its doors to advanced students and offered them an education in which, according to President Daniel Coit Gilman, the sciences would stand on equal footing with the humanities, which had too long enjoyed exalted status at English colleges.

In Baltimore in 1876, Thomas Huxley, the contentious English biologist, applauded Gilman's decision, and, moreover, he advised the Hopkins' trustees not to follow English architectural practices either, not to erect Gothic quadrangles, but, rather, to have none but simple, economical, serviceable buildings designed and erected by "an honest brick-layer."[16] Huxley's advice agreed with the wishes of Gilman and of scientists generally, who held mechanistic function in high regard; a typical result of their beliefs was the Ward Pavilion at the Johns Hopkins University Hospital. Erected about 1888 (plate 2), it was a severely functional, efficient machine, but it resembled an ugly moraine, in brick.

Fearful lest the glacier of expedient functionalism should scour the American landscape, professional architects and their clients imported classic and medieval architectural styles, naïvely hoping to summon art by borrowing what was time-honored, but already out-worn, in Europe. In 1875, for example, Abner Jackson, President of Trinity College, was confronted with the task of having to find an architect to design a new campus. His College at Hartford was a liberal arts institution on the English model, and Jackson declared his intellectual lineage by travelling immediately to England, where William Burges, a Victorian Gothic architect, attracted his attention. Burges designed a totally unrealistic phantasy for Trinity, a college he had never seen, in a land he had never visited.

Such blind reliance on Europe had been, inevitably, a Colonial condition, but long after political independence had been won the cultural chains remained. By 1800, even immigrant architects like Benjamin Latrobe, from England, rallied for something indigenous, hoping (vainly, as it turned out) for an architecture related to the wants and means of the United States. Unfortunately too many Americans followed the amateur example of Thomas Jefferson who, though he respected Latrobe's advice on practical matters, insisted upon covering the brilliantly serviceable site plan for the University of Virginia with temple fronts Jefferson copied from books illustrating Roman and Palladian architecture. Such misapplied scholarship ferried the pagan classic image along the riverways, canals and postroads until the Civil War; then, the purveyors of cultivated taste became infatuated by John Ruskin, and that Englishman's sermons in favor of the Gothic Revival rolled mid-west on the rails and sailed to California around the Horn.

Inspired by Ruskin, a group in New York, the Association for the Advancement of Truth in Art, trumpeted for Gothic as a moral, truthful, Christian architecture, consistent with its curious interpretation of America's heritage. The Association's greatest triumph was the National Academy of Design at New York, by Peter Bonnett Wight, who shared Ruskin's belief that architecture had a messianic duty to promote moral behavior.[17] Perhaps the epitome of America's flirtation with Ruskin was visible at Cambridge in 1875, where William Ware, together with his partner, Henry Van Brunt, was watching their plans unfold in Harvard's Memorial Hall (plate 3), a Victorian Gothic Civil War monument, resembling a cathedral. Guided by Harvard's art critic, Charles Eliot Norton, Memorial Hall in its early stages, at least, had received the benign approval of Ruskin, so Professor Norton liked to recall.

America's schism in taste—Harvard's Memorial Hall, Hopkins' Ward Pavilion —struck Sullivan as a basic antipathy needing to be resolved: " . . . the attenuated vulgarity of pseudo-culture versus the savage vulgarity of rowdyism."[18]

THE FERMENT IN CHICAGO

Certainly, the resolution had not yet been accomplished in Chicago. For an industrial baron, architects leafed through the pages of César Daly's *Architecture privée du XIXe siècle,* published in 1864, to find suggestions for palaces, like Potter Palmer's which John M. Van Osdel concocted in the ornate, mansarded vogue of France's Second Empire. The engineer, William le Baron Jenney, was erecting small, pitifully emasculated Gothic churches, and so was Burnham & Root, despite the triumphs this young firm later achieved.

Meanwhile, among the many bald and perfunctory warehouses, factories and office buildings, there were examples of progress in engineering, such as the hollow tile, fireproof floors George H. Johnson built into his Kendall Building in 1872, and there was Frederick Baumann's theory for intermittent supports for buildings, announced in his book, *A Theory of Isolated Pier Foundations,* published in 1873.

Thus, in 1875, the two points of view—archaeology or science, heritage or progress, foreign orientation or indigenous resourcefulness—either stood side by side confronting each other, or their conflict was buried, usually by forcing the engineer to prop any historical form the architect suggested.

But already in the mid-seventies Chicago was in ferment. Typically, when Peter Bonnett Wight was unable to find further work at New York, he moved west, abandoned his Ruskinian sympathy for Italian Gothic, manufactured fireproof tile, and wrote approvingly of Chicago's functional warehouses and factories. In 1878, the Eastern *American Architect* continued to klaxon for the use of mixed, archaeological styles and spoke of Americans, in the day of the melting-pot, as the lucky " . . . heirs of all the treasures of the Old World. . . . "[19] In the following year, a new magazine, *The Western Architect and Builder,* was founded to champion the vernacular architecture of St. Louis and Chicago.

That journal occasionally reflected the fascinating speculation, proposed by the French historian and critic, Viollet-le-Duc, that a new architecture might rise upon a structure of iron, a possibility that Americans saw brilliantly forecast in Joseph Paxton's Crystal Palace at London in 1851 (plate 4). Viollet-le-Duc's advocacy of an architecture that expressed its metal structural system was a clear call for a non-historical way of building, and Chicagoans began speaking of it as "structural realism" and "rational building" (plate 5).

Such calls for realism were racing around in young Western heads when Sullivan, aged 19, struck up a friendship with the engineer, Frederick Baumann. Sullivan became interested in engineering, watched Baumann's work with the new foundations, studied Trautwine's *Engineer's Pocket Bible,* and followed the accounts of the construction of Eads' trussed iron bridge at St. Louis. Next, he came under the tutelage of the architect, John Edelmann, who encouraged Sullivan to read widely. Sullivan himself had already read Taine's *Philosophy of Art;* now he studied John Tyndall's *Fragments of Science,* Darwin's *Origin of Species,* and, at Edelmann's suggestion, explored Spencer, Rabelais, Shakespeare and Swinburne. But the diverse ideas remained unsynthesized, as did the diverse tendencies in Sullivan's architectural thinking before 1890—a period largely of structural realism and picturesque ornament, which he regarded as preparatory, his summer of inspiration.

His friendship with Edelmann also launched Sullivan in architectural practice. Through him, Sullivan obtained a commission to design the decoration for Edelmann's Sinai Synagogue, followed by frescoes, on a botanical theme, he painted for Edelmann's Moody Tabernacle.[20] Again through Edelmann, in 1879, Sullivan met Dankmar Adler, who since his years as an engineer during the Civil War had developed a following in Chicago among clients who respected his practical knowledge and technical ingenuity in building. Sullivan joined his office when Adler was doing the indifferent Central Music Hall (1879), which resembled the American Express Company Building (plate 6), a picturesque commercial palace by the Eastern architect Henry Hobson Richardson. Sullivan so successfully complemented his talents that Adler developed complete, implicit faith in the young artist, and a new partnership, Adler & Sullivan, was formed in 1881.

SULLIVAN'S EARLY BUILDINGS

Their early work strove for individuality and picturesqueness and was derivative and fractious. Their residences, for example, exhibit Victorian aesthetic values, visible in the row of three houses Adler built for himself, his mother-in-law and Eli B. Felsenthal on Ellis Avenue in 1885–86 (plate 7). Massive blocks with fantastic skylines, their façades are broken by irregular rhythms and accents in oriels, bays and gables. Impressionistic fracturing of volumes produced broken, rustic surfaces, patchworks in varied colors and textures, and an efflorescence of ornament at cornices, in gables, on flat surfaces, and in capitals and railings. While such furtive individual variations upon a residential type might have richly and gracefully enclosed the perimeter of a fine park, the large scale of urban scenery was not approached by Sullivan; nor can one imagine a successful transfer of his "Queen Anne" picturesqueness to a monumental urban building.

For example, the residences suggested no answer to the most fascinating problem, the office building. Here, the early efforts were tentative, scattered in their aims and generally unsuccessful. Essentially, the problem had two parts; there was the group of technical problems: how to utilize iron so that the tall building would be least heavy, how to anchor it in Chicago's mud, and how to give it the light, air, heat and mechanical circulation its occupants required; second, there were the aesthetic problems: how to express the iron structure in the exterior fireproof cladding and how to unify the composition by using proportions, scale, rhythms and ornament that were appropriate to its size and functions. Those problems of rational building and structural realism had not yet been solved anywhere, not even in Richardson's American Express Company Building; nor would Sullivan solve them during the eighties.

The tall commercial building fascinated and perplexed Sullivan. In his Borden Block (1879–80) (plate 8), a technically advanced system of construction enabled thick brick piers to subdivide the wall into bays of wide, light-giving windows, which were set between thin cast-iron spandrels and mullions; but horizontal string courses detracted from the Block's verticality, while redundant structural elements gave a picayune scale. The Rothschild Store (1880–81) (plate 9), headed toward the vertical theme, and window areas expanded so that the wall was a series of mullions that were exceedingly slender and continuously vertical. Obviously Sullivan was feeling his way toward distinguishing the pier from the mullion, but the Rothschild's arresting clutter of brittle cast-iron ornament was diversionary. Such diversions also marred the Revell Building (1881–83), where the bays are disposed in a stuttering manner (plate 10). Sullivan's bias was toward exotic ornament, as in the deceptively scaled Ryerson Building (1884) (plate 11), whose armature of iron was blasphemed by squat piers and irrelevant ornament.

On a different tack, Sullivan next sought a simpler, horizontal expression. His Troescher Building (1884) (plate 12) offered an enormous clarification which was achieved by projecting plain, continuous brick piers in front of wide, recessed spandrels; but the summit was a disappointingly turgid recall of the arches in the base. Although the Troescher's more geometric and better unified ornament suited the realistic statement of structure, Sullivan began to avoid the problem.

Forthright bareness characterized especially his factories. Particularly noteworthy is his Shoe Factory for Selz Schwab and Company (1886–87), which gains monumentality through its stately rhythms in a structure that is factually expressed; taken merely as a planar wall, it is not without refinements, notably the low-arched, brick spandrels, which relieve the stark angularity of piers, themselves tapered so that reveals are gradually diminished in the upper stories (plate 13). Yet structural logic alone did not satisfy the artist who once said, " . . . I should not wish to see a rose reduced to the syllogism. . . . "[21]

Remarkably, Sullivan refused to approach his problems archaeologically, but, as yet, he had not found his own medium. His contemporary, John Wellborn Root, correctly remarked in 1890, "So exuberant is he that he sometimes seems to neglect the larger questions of mass, of light and shade, of sky-blotch, in his care for delicacy, beauty and significance of detail. . . . "[22] Evidently Sullivan could achieve fine passages of structural realism in a single wall, as in the factory, but he had not yet grasped an architectural expression of masses and spaces, and he relied upon picturesque, elaborate ornament to lend notes of individuality and originality, as though such Romantic values were related to quality.

In fact, Adler & Sullivan's fame was built on Chicago's Auditorium (1886–89), which displayed their technical prowess, their indecision as yet about aesthetics. The idea for an auditorium began with the successful Opera Festival in the Spring, 1885, which inspired its sponsor, Ferdinand W. Peck, to organize support for a permanent opera house for theater, balls, symphony concerts, and political conventions; to make it pay, he decided to include a commercial hotel and business offices. Peck's confidence in Adler's knowledge of acoustics, mechanical equipment, and circulation brought the commission to Adler & Sullivan in the summer of 1886. The *parti* was soon decided: a theater surrounded by a shell of hotel rooms, with business offices located in a tower over the theater entrance.

Adler mastered each technical problem: 4,237 seats were located in the parquet, main balcony and two galleries; to gain good acoustics, the parquet was sloped upward seventeen feet, and four elliptical arches were thrown across the space; mechanical equipment was hidden in a large plenum beneath the stage, where pumps, hydraulic rams, and engines for the curtains, cyclorama and ventilation were all accessible; large spaces accommodated the Congress Street entrance to the theater and the Michigan Avenue entrance to the hotel; interior supports were cast-iron columns, and the exterior walls were solid brick, a massively heavy construction, which might have settled unevenly had Adler not ingeniously loaded the tower concurrently with the wall in proportion to their foundations' ultimate loads.

Meanwhile, a sequence of perspectives for the Auditorium tellingly recorded Sullivan's struggles. An early design (plate 14), a fractious mass, lacked any constancy of motif, rhythm, scale or structure; its squat tower failed in proportions, and picturesque pips cropped out all over the bulky mass. The second design, also drawn in 1886, (plate 15) grasped the geometric block, but its scale was still picayune, its rhythms never emerged clearly, and its major divisions were still clouded by sentimentalities and trivialities. In one of those strokes that seemed a calamity then and a virtue now, economics forced Sullivan to omit much exterior flourish, and the building emerged more nearly a sheer, clifflike mass—a three-storied base of heavily rusticated granite supporting noble rhythms in the arcade above.

Indeed, one senses in the final composition a movement away from rational expression. On the interior (plate 17), for example, the great arches that bridge the magnificently ornamented theater help to create the superb space, and they seem to be the structural supports for the ceiling; actually the ceiling was hung from exterior iron trusses, and the arched diaphragms were built to serve as acoustic baffles and deflectors; they also have an incidental function in housing ventilation ducts, but their chief importance is acoustical and spatial, and they symbolize Adler & Sullivan's decisive departure from structural realism.

Moreover, the exterior massing does not literally tell the disposition of interior functions (plate 19). Changes in motif, direction, and texture separate elements that serve identical functions, and, elsewhere, different interior uses are not given distinguishing expressions on the exterior. Rather than rational literalism, the composition of the mass aimed at unified, geometric clarity, as all great architecture has.

As yet, disunity remains: the tower makes no inflection as it joins the building; the balcony off the hotel parlor on Michigan Avenue is a disturbing, elephantine accent; the proportion of the base is too high; and the vertical rhythm of stories is uninteresting because of its dull symmetry. But, those blemishes occur within a composition that was better unified than the "truthful" statements of function that cluttered Sullivan's early buildings with myriad solecisms.

What monumentality the Auditorium had, it owed to its aesthetic organization, not to its structure, which was traditional. That it was structurally timid, if not retrogressive, we may recall by mentioning the Home Insurance Company Building (1884), where Jenney pioneered the use of metal skeletal construction, a technical, though not in Jenney's hands an aesthetic, treasure. Had the Auditorium really driven toward the new possibilities, it would have followed the suggestions Burnham & Root offered in their Rookery Building, where the metal skeleton beautifully organized the interior walls of the court.

But the Auditorium, instead, surpassed both of those technically progressive structures by virtue of its massing. Its chief features followed suggestions offered by Richardson, the Boston architect, who popularized the Romanesque Revival.

In the year before his premature death, Richardson arrived in Chicago to design some houses and also one important commercial building, the Marshall Field Wholesale Warehouse (1885–87); it was Chicago's first look at grand composition (plate 22). Its superb rhythms, its stately arcades, its rich surfaces, its decisive geometry, its serene mass—all carried on a traditional structural system—were in marked contrast to the turgidity of Sullivan and the banal, confused outpourings of engineers like Jenney, however technically progressive they were. Thus, as had happened before and would happen again, the strongest aesthetic statement occurred within a structurally retrogressive building, whose suggestions regarding form invited transfer and universal application.

Sullivan declared his admiration for Richardson in a series of buildings: Chicago's Standard Club (1887–89); the Heath residence, built in Chicago in 1889; and the Opera House Block (1890) in Pueblo, Colorado; none was impressive, except perhaps the Dooly Block in Salt Lake City (1890–91) (plate 23), whose arcaded piers and recessed spandrels literally recalled Richardson's building. Only the Walker Warehouse (1888–89) (plates 24–26), in Chicago's Loop, offered a significant development; its voids cut precisely into a clean, cubic silhouette, which was devoid of any ornament and bounded by planes.

Although he might have admitted that Richardson had taught him the important lesson of geometric clarity, if you had asked Sullivan in 1890 whether his Walker Warehouse satisfied him, he would have replied that it did not. For he had not yet come to terms with the steel skeleton, and, meanwhile, Jenney, in his Second Leiter Building (1889–90), and Burnham & Root, in their Reliance Building (begun in 1890), had created sheer crystals of glass held in steel webs (plate 27). Those were highly advanced examples of structural realism, but they did not quench Sullivan's thirst for emotional expression, and his insight into organic growth now demanded something superior.

3. AUTUMN GLORY

ALL THAT Sullivan had achieved thus far was preparatory to his mastery of the tall building after 1890. Again theory marched alongside practice. Everyone had recognized the practical problems: to support a ten-story building, fireproof throughout, accessible by swift elevators, with batteries of boilers supplying energy for pumps, ventilation fans, electric dynamos; a building flooded with light, hung on a steel cage, and subdivided by terra-cotta partitions. Even Henry Van Brunt, codesigner of Harvard's Memorial Hall, now renounced his early preference for Gothic: " . . . such a problem," he wrote from Chicago in 1889, "does not call for the same sort of architectural inspiration as the building of a vaulted cathedral in the Middle Ages. . . . "[23]

PLEAS FOR UNITY AND A NEW STYLE

But mere factual recognition of the practical problems was no longer satisfactory.

Viollet-le-Duc's structural realism, the engineer's rational planning—both were insufficient bases for great architecture. Proof of their inadequacy was visible in St. Louis' Fagin Building (1889), where realistic and rational shafts were uncouth barbarisms that terminated in rowdy boulders above; according to a writer in the *Architectural Record,* the Fagin attempted to make " . . . slovenliness, profanity and profuse expectoration signs of force of character."[24]

National taste now wanted buildings in which the elements of architecture—mass, space and plane—were adjusted by principles of balance, rhythm, scale and proportion to effect unity, even if structural facts and logical planning should become subordinated, if not belied. Typical of the pleas was John Beverly Robinson's book, *Principles of Architectural Composition* (1899), while the fountainhead of the theories, Julien Guadet's *Eléments et théories d'architecture,* appeared in Paris in 1901. Both writers recognized that aesthetic unity is independent of style, that style fluctuates as the elements of architecture—notably structural systems—change in accordance with a society's technology, economics and beliefs. The hallmark of formal quality rests in compositional unity, while style gives expressive power, telling when and by whom a building was built. Unfortunately, the distinction between composition and style was too often misunderstood, and then voices that were laudably raised in favor of perfecting form wrongly spoke as though Classic style alone were the source of majesty. That clearly was the misinterpretation proffered by many American architects in the early twentieth century, and their monuments to an uninformed taste were enthusiastically accepted by clients.

Perhaps Sullivan learned the roles of composition and style from Beaux-Arts theory at the Ecole; more likely, the impetus toward formal unity comes to all mature architects, as it had to Richardson, also a Beaux-Arts student, as it would, and tryrannically, to Wright, who eschewed academic theory, at least in his words. By 1890, Sullivan was seeking a principle of composition or, as he preferred to speak of it, an organization with a grammar expressive of his society.

He avidly pursued the hints at a new style offered by European writers, whose calls to boldness were translated and printed in Chicago's magazine, *The Inland Architect and News Record.* In 1890, for example, Chicagoans read César Daly's thrust at eclecticism, a thrust sprung from the Hegelian principle that each age has its own form of expression: "Each style of architecture, being born of the intellectual and moral forces of a human society . . . , has become naturally the expression of a certain civilization. . . . The adoption by one age of a style . . . other than that which it has itself created, is hence in itself a false principle."[25] Significantly, Sullivan's friend, the progressive architect John Wellborn Root, translated a similar message written by the German, Gottfried Semper, who referred to "Darwin's doctrine of evolutions," then said: "Building styles . . . are not invented, but develop . . . from a few primitive types . . . similar to the evolutions in the province of organic creation."[26] Pointed in its similarity to Sullivan's ideas is Semper's statement, "The old monuments are . . . fossil shells of extinct organisms of society. . . . Style is the conformity of an art object with the circumstances of its origin and . . . its development."[27]

Thus, about 1890 the theory of architecture as organic adaptation and organic expression gripped Chicagoans. Architects engaged in heated discussions. At one meeting Sullivan joined Baumann, Root and Adler to discuss "the present tendencies of architectural design in America." Baumann wanted to emphasize utility: "What is style?" he asked, and quoted Semper, "Style is the coincidence of a structure with the conditions of its origin."[28] Sullivan protested that the discussion had started entirely at the wrong end, and the participants thereupon charged him with having to present a paper for discussion. At a subsequent meeting he spoke of the pine tree, its tapering trunk, its branching, its hold on the rocks, its bark, leaves, flowers, cones, seeds and sap, each of which is characterizing: The style of a pine tree "is the resultant of its identity and its surroundings. . . . The style is ever thus the response of the organism to the surroundings."[29]

The idea of organism, which connotes organization into a whole function or purpose, is an old idea, and it has generally received either a mechanistic or a vital interpretation. An organism may be organized like a machine; translated into architectural terms, a mechanistic emphasis implies the ascendency of physical function, efficient circulation, structural strength and truthful expression of materials. But there is also a romantic aspect of organic expression, which refers to an individual's will to achieve greater vitality, especially for the imagination and emotions, with a consequent premium placed upon the individual, his humanity and equality, in which man's relation to his environment, both physical and social, becomes paramount.

Both aspects of the theory, stemming from roots in the eighteenth century, appeared early in America, notably in the criticism written by Horatio Greenough about 1840 and also in the writings of Emerson, who approved of Coleridge's statement, "The organic form . . . is innate; it shapes, as it develops, itself from within. . . . "[30] That background is significant because Sullivan greatly admired Emerson, as well as Whitman, including their calls to a self-reliant nationalism.

Sullivan's principle was summarized in his often-quoted and much-abused dictum, " . . . *form follows function* . . . ,"[31] first announced in 1895. His *Autobiography* mentioned some of the progenitors of that important idea: "In Darwin he found much food. The Theory of Evolution seemed stupendous."[32] And he firmly intended to consider society as an organism, following "Spencer's definition implying a progression from an unorganized simple, through stages of growth and differentiation to a highly organized complex. . . . "[33] Both the Darwinian and the Spencerian aspects are important, for Sullivan believed that a building must express the environment from which it develops, both the physical and the social aspects of that environment.

There were five essential features in Sullivan's idea. First, the process of creating architecture must be natural in being intuitive. Rational principles and formulas, he constantly avowed, were dangerous things: " . . . we, in our art, are to follow Nature's processes, Nature's rhythms, because those processes, those rhythms, are vital, organic, coherent, logical above all book logic. . . . "[34] Second, architecture must necessarily evolve from and express the environment from which it grows; it must be adapted to it. Adaptation naturally tended to glorify the present, including, for Sullivan's period, modern technology and industry and, especially, democracy, as a characteristic of the American environment; he sought a modern, national, democratic architecture and hated the Classic because, for him, it seemed aristocratic. Third, good architecture must express its own particular function; fourth, it must be truthful to its structure and purpose; and fifth, it must seek expression in ornament based on natural growth.[35] The five requirements constituted Sullivan's polemic on style, a theory about life, really, now transferred to building so that architecture would become what Sullivan believed it to be—a social manifestation.

A NEW STYLE TREATED CLASSICALLY

Masterly evidence of Sullivan's arrival appeared in three buildings he designed during the year 1890. Two stood at opposite poles of social purpose: a warehouse and a tomb. Customarily such contrasting uses would have been expressed by a hierarchy of styles—Gothic or Classic for the commemorative; purely expedient and utilitarian for the commercial. Sullivan cut through the hierarchy with one forceful synthesis. The Cold Storage Exchange Warehouse (1891) (plate 28) brilliantly handled the problems of access by ship, train, tramway and wagon, and its monumentality was a function of justly placed masses, stately rhythms, sober scale, and cliff-like walls. He did not change his stride to design the Getty Tomb (1890) (plates 29–32) at Chicago's Graceland Cemetery. The heavy cornice presses down upon a noble mass of gray limestone; symmetrical organization and serene balance frame the beautifully ornamental bronze gates (plate 30). Between the two expressions stood the Anshe Ma'ariv Synagogue (plates 33–35), which combines useful with commemorative purposes. Begun in 1890, the building unfortunately flagrantly departed from the drawings Sullivan made for it, but its truncated mass and large entrance were intended to be compelling invitations to enter a dramatic space whose splendor had been withheld from the passersby.

The skeptic will rightly ask whether the three buildings have anything to do with Sullivan's theory, and the candid critic must readily offer an opinion that has long been stifled by some historians who understood Sullivan partially and treated him as one who anticipated German mechanistic architecture but, unfortunately, still suffered from nineteenth-century devotions to picturesque towers and ornament.[36] That interpretation fails to recognize that Sullivan's theory proposed a vital, not merely a mechanistic, organization.

Moreover, it was a theory about style, and Sullivan's buildings reflect some parts of it, but not all. To the extent that each is original, the buildings conform to Sullivan's insistence upon natural processes for creation and his acceptance of that modern fetish for innovation which prizes uniqueness above all else (even at the expense of preventing the perfecting of an idea through repeated efforts at improvement). The buildings also exhibit his ambition to remain faithful to structure and purpose and to make ornament an abstraction from nature's examples.

The troublesome aspect of the theory rests in its call for expression of environment. The Getty Tomb is not a testimonial to modern technology; one would be hard put to defend the thesis that Synagogue is democratic; and the Warehouse's claim to being American can be thrown into doubt by a mere glance at comparable structures in England and Germany. The fact is that Sullivan's buildings, theory or not, were not so much expressions of his society as they were declarations of what that society should stand for; his art, like all art, did not rest upon fidelity of representation: it was myth-making, and it shared with earlier architectures such forceful organizations as symmetry, which Sullivan did not discuss in his theory because, unlike Richardson and Wright (who often achieved remarkable successes with occult balances), Sullivan sought not new principles of composition, but rather a new style, an ornamented expression of the rhythms suggested by new structural systems; and he intended to compose them classically, in keeping with his desire for repose.

Indeed, one notes the greater serenity in Sullivan's buildings, the peace he attained after the exhausting struggle with the Auditorium. He particularly associated that calmness with Ocean Springs, Mississippi, where he built a simple cottage for himself in 1890 (plate 38). There, on the sleepy backwaters of Biloxi Bay, his retreat stood among pines, azaleas, and wistaria; his rose garden offered him respite from the striving city: " . . . to remain unperturbed and serene within this turbulent and drifting flow of hope and sorrow . . . is the uttermost position and fact attainable to the soul. . . . "[37] He wrote that inspiration was killed by the city and came from solitude in the country alone. "Nature," he said, " . . . is the source of power; and the city, the arena in which that power is dissipated. . . . "[38]

Yet, Sullivan remained urbane, and his architecture was an urban architecture even if he did not propose a plan for reorganizing cities. His lineage lay in the sophisticated Western civic tradition, and, despite his paeans to the rural life, Sullivan did not build for the agrarian setting; nor did he draw upon the primitive, prehistoric or rustic sources that fed the imagination of his apprentice, Frank Lloyd Wright.

How much Wright contributed to Sullivan's development will never be known exactly, but the relation between "der lieber Meister" and the young Wright, who joined him in 1887 and soon became his chief draftsman, reversed the usual apprenticeship, just as the young Leonardo had affected the older Verrocchio. We see a new personality emerging in the work of Adler & Sullivan, and by 1891 that personality had declared itself in the Charnley House (plate 40), where each feature asserts the level line. Its severe rectangles avoid all whimsy and complexity in favor of repose. Wright became an increasingly strong force, and some of the inconsistent verticalities and horizontalities that may be detected seem to indicate what Grant Manson has called "an uneasy union of Celts."[39]

Their association terminated in 1893 when Wright was incensed by Sullivan's refusal to sanction his designing "boot-legged houses" at Oak Park. But the break was inevitable if either personality was to develop: Wright's toward a rural architecture of dynamic spaces and masses composed asymmetrically, Sullivan's toward urban reserve and classic composure. For Sullivan's dedications lay on the axis from Athens to Rome to Paris; though Goths and Celts might alter its structural systems and change its ornament, the heritage was Western, civic and classic, as Sullivan's admiration for Michelangelo attested.

Indeed, Sullivan's buildings of 1892–93 show pronounced development toward classic organization within his coherent, highly individual style. A residence for his brother, Albert, is subdivided into base, wall and heavy cornice (plate 41); the wall is a smooth Palladian plane sharply incised by the crisp cuts made for doors and windows, though the oriel is a fossil left from the earlier attempts at picturesque plasticity. More classical still, the Wainwright Tomb (1892) (plate 42), in Bellefontaine Cemetery, St. Louis, is a pantheon whose low dome covers a sanctuary decorated with dark blue mosaic. Again in the classic mode, Sullivan's Transportation Building for the Columbian Exposition at Chicago in 1893 was a Beaux-Arts composition (plates 43, 44), and not a happy one either, though it gained undeserved reputation as a masterpiece because its style did not conform to the Classical buildings at the Fair. The famous Golden Door, an isolated fragment which stood in front of a shed, was not lacking in unhappy zigzag scrolls and irrelevant kiosks; but it was awarded three medals by French architects, who claimed that Sullivan alone among Americans understood what the Ecole had taught.

It was his synthesis of traditional composition with a new style, notably his proportions, rhythms and ornament—all consistent with skeletal structures—that Sullivan brought to the tall commercial building. Aesthetic form appropriate to the skyscraper first appeared in Sullivan's Wainwright Building (plates 45–49), erected in St. Louis in 1890–91. Built on a U-shaped plan, with the court facing north, the Wainwright contains stores on its ground floor and offices above them. Classical organization phrases the elevations in three parts: a two-foot base of red Missouri granite supports two stories of finely jointed brown sandstone; above, red-brick piers rise continuously from the third to the tenth stories; the top story and cornice terminate the shaft with a blaze of ornament, made in red terra cotta. Seen early on a Spring morning with its summit crested by a red sun, as it appeared the first time I saw it, the Wainwright is the very token of the silted Mississippi flowing near-by.

Yet its shape is by no means a frank revelation of interior functions or supports. Mullions that lack steel are not differentiated from the piers which do the work. The base includes both stores and offices, though the mezzanine, realistically, should have been treated like the third story. The corner piers are over seven feet wide, though their steel sustains no increased load that justifies the magnification. The wide overhanging cornice serves no practical function, and the ornamented frieze at the tenth story shields nothing more graceful than mechanical equipment. All those departures from functional expression were intended to translate physical fact into aesthetic reality. In the determination of aesthetic form, the principles of proportion, rhythm, termination, balance and scale were essential, just as structural solidity and logical planning were necessary to useful form. Sullivan's quest demanded all three measures, but not equal expression of them.

Great as it was, the Wainwright must be regarded as a partial triumph. Its spaces are serviceable but not wonderful, and no large master space provides a reference point for the corridors and small offices. Even the light court, which might have been graceful, does not capitalize upon the façade's pier and spandrel motif, though Wright later showed how it might be used to enclose a handsome court inside his Larkin Building at Buffalo. Sullivan at the Wainwright, it must be admitted, displayed his mastery of mass, of rhythm, of magnificient ornament; his walls sustain prolonged, enjoyable scrutiny because their major lines are emphatically simple, and their carpet of dense, red ornament varies in the spandrels at each floor; but, unlike recent modern architects, he was not principally concerned with magnificent spaces.

Rather, he strove for a soaring, slender, free-standing tower or slab. His second skyscraper, the Schiller Building (1891–92) in Chicago, was a seventeen-story tower emphasized by long, continuous piers, but still encumbered by horizontal distractions and not yet permitted to stand free (plate 50). An unexecuted design, Fraternity Temple (plate 51), published in 1891, was more prescient. Remarkable for its imaginative suggestions of a skyscraper for an urban setting, a thirty-five story tower was depicted as arising from the center of a cross formed by four twenty-one story buildings, two of which were joined by ten-story slabs that stood parallel with the central block. The envelope declared its need for light, and its diminished mass in the upper stories revealed Sullivan's belief that the skyscraper should not be allowed to crowd out all air and light and become a "social menace and danger."[40] His design was a far-seeing anticipation of the zoning laws that later curbed exploitations of *laissez-faîre* land coverage, envelope-filling and unbridled height; but Sullivan received no mandate to build accordingly.

After still another bountiful but undeveloped suggestion, the corrugated wall surface in Chicago's Stock Exchange (1893–94) (plates 52, 53), Sullivan returned to the Wainwright's format for his best skyscraper, Buffalo's Guaranty (later Prudential) Building (1894–95), whose genesis was discussed earlier (plates 54–64). Its tall mass, with a light court at the rear, seems to be raised above the ground on columns; above the mezzanine, the piers are doubled, indicating that only alternate ones contain steel, and they terminate in an arcade. A rich play of surface ornament, in red and green terra-cotta sheathing, covers both structural and nonbearing members and spreads across the cornice. Inflections, rhythms, terminations and scale handsomely isolate the monumental slab. There exists, perhaps, one unsatisfactory compromise at the ground story, where the plate glass projects past the columns (plate 58); the device served to expose the capitals, gain full space for displays of merchandise, and eliminate reflections by bringing light behind the glass, but it disturbs the orderly statement of wall and column with a blemish that, for some critics, enhances character in a form that is otherwise perfectly composed and splendidly ornamented.

How far Sullivan had now progressed can best be seen by contrasting his buildings to those of contemporary Chicago realists. His Gage Building (1898–99), for example, was built to stand as one of three buildings on Michigan Avenue (plates 65–67). Two were designed by Holabird & Roche. Their handling of the pier, spandrel and large window is laudable, but their compositions are marred by dualities, strange endings, grossness, and misalignments; obviously, they had found a formula for fenestration and kept to it. The Gage Building, however, states a delicate, measured cadence; perhaps the door's location is worrisome; perhaps the ground floor protests: but the façade springs forth in a lively manner, and its ornament is entirely appropriate to its feminine purpose, a milliner's showcase. If the Gage still does not seem especially "natural," especially "democratic," especially "American," its architecture went beyond the rational and the realistic; its harmonious expression may well serve as the symbol for American aspirations in the late nineteenth century, for it united technology with art, science with an emotional faith in what was inscrutably vital.

4. *WINTER PESSIMISM*

DESPITE HIS ACHIEVEMENT, cynical bitterness crept upon Louis Sullivan about 1900 when events conspired to affect his fortune adversely; he succumbed to despondency and felt himself a failure. His disappointments began with his family. Always a keen observer of people, Sullivan's scrutiny bared a man's ambitious character and prevented close friendships with few except his family. After his father's death in 1885, his mother's in 1892, Sullivan's long intimacy with his brother was impaired, and Albert's marriage in 1892 with a possessive, hypercritical woman who jealously alienated former friends brought an estrangement between the two brothers.

The Panic of 1893 decreased commissions, and the less prosperous partnership, Adler & Sullivan, hit hard times. The firm was dissolved in 1895 when Adler insisted upon admitting his two sons as partners. Adler had won the confidence of clients, he commanded impressive technical knowledge, and the admirable spaces in the Auditorium and Synagogue suggest that he, not Sullivan, may have had the better understanding of circulation and space, for Sullivan's buildings in the years after the partnership was broken seldom contain spaces as memorable, though he became more masterful in his wall patterns, fenestration and ornament.

Sullivan, unfortunately, does not seem to have recognized Adler's contributions; his self-confidence was elated by his work at Buffalo and by French encomiums. In a day when commerce asked that large firms of specialist architects be organized to produce standard designs quickly and in large numbers, Sullivan chose not to enter another partnership, and he suffered the consequences of remaining an artist who worked individually upon a few choice buildings.

While he was still hopeful, with commissions at New York and Chicago, Sullivan met a divorcee whom he married in 1899. But work dwindled, his marriage was unhappy, he drank heavily, and his wife left him in 1906. Over all hung his humiliation; society, it seemed, had passed him by.

THE SPECTER OF THE FAIR

Sullivan was bound to fare poorly among people who applauded the commercial architect, seldom the artist. Rewards went to the man who was reliable technically and financially, provided he did not offend taste by suggesting aesthetic innovations, provided his architectural commonplaces became emblems of social prestige. The national hero was surely Daniel Burnham—master organizer of the World's Columbian Exposition of 1893, international champion of the Fair's Classic architecture.

Burnham became Sullivan's arch-symbol of the prevailing order: intent on bigness at a time of mergers, combinations and trusts; a manager of efficient organizations where success bred success; a politician in a day of large contracts from governments and corporations; an urban planner in a day of city reform; and purveyor of a commercialized Classic style. "It is not good policy," Burnham once told Sullivan, "to go much above the general level of intelligence."[41] Typically, Burnham ridiculed a young draftsman's attempt at daring design. "What is your authority for that?" asked Burnham. "*I* am," replied the brazen youth. "It is original." "Oh!" said Burnham, "Get a good authority."[42]

As the memory of Burnham's Fair carried the Great White City idea nationally, Sullivan bitterly attacked it as a "lewd exhibit of drooling imbecility and political debauchery."[43] His *Autobiography* reached its climax in his revelation of the organic idea, then plummeted to its conclusion at the time of the Fair when " . . . Architecture died in the land of the free. . . . "[44] Sullivan saw Burnham and his Eastern friends default in the dilemma the Fair had proposed to Henry Adams; they neglected both the Dynamo and the Virgin and paid their homage to Venus.

Sullivan stubbornly refused to ingratiate himself, played the part of the Carlylean hero whose times do not heed him, lost commissions by refusing to concede even on incidental points, and remained more Wagnerian in his hopes for triumph than in his personal strength to avoid self-pity in defeat. Commissions dwindled to about twenty in his last twenty-nine years, as contrasted to more than one hundred in the period before 1895. Occasionally still he showed that his talent remained, especially in two buildings of about 1900 when he was supremely confident of the future.

New York acquired its lone example of Sullivan's genius in 1897–98 when the twelve-story Bayard, later called Condict, Building raised its steel frame on Bleecker Street (plates 68–71). Its organization of pier, mullion and spandrel, its splendid ornament and tracery in terra cotta, gave New York its first suggestion of form appropriate to the skyscraper; but the drive toward Classicism could not be retarded, and New Yorkers soon called Burnham to erect his Fuller Building, a wedge-shaped block organized like a Doric column (plate 79).

Meanwhile, Sullivan gained his greatest opportunity, a commission from the Schlesinger & Mayer Company in Chicago. Their department store had long occupied the strategic corner where State crosses Madison Street. Sullivan's new building was perfectly formed to exploit that location (plate 72). The first unit was erected beginning in 1899, and a second, higher unit was added in 1903–04, after which the flourishing business was purchased by Carson Pirie Scott & Company who continue to occupy Sullivan's building. Generous display and sales areas were made to stand on large, nearly uninterrupted floors, and they receive abundant light, made possible by the steel frame of skyscraper construction. The resultant interior spaces are commercially serviceable, but they have no architectural distinction. Their characterlessness is compensated for by the impression the store makes from the street: a series of large showcases that relentlessly beckon to the pedestrian and cause him to linger at displays of dresses, suits or sweaters. The entire surface is a continuous membrane, with maximum fenestration set in piers and spandrels that stand nearly on the same plane (plate 75). The two-story base is sheathed in a casing of ornamental iron, fabulous for its intricate scrolls of leafy ornament, which set the displays in *mille fleurs* tapestries of arresting, nearly Celtic, interlaced leaves (plates 76, 77).

The ornamented, horizontal fenestration tends to hold the pedestrian's eyes to the displays, but the modern architect's eye also enjoys being forced to the upper stories, where the fenestration stands clarion clear (plate 74). A reduction in the height of the top three stories marks an interesting but not damaging concession to economy, and their pattern originally was terminated at the twelfth story by an overhanging roof, which cast heavy shadows upon the band of deeply recessed windows.

Not long ago, when a stringent, mechanistic functionalism dominated in architecture, the upper sections of the store were more admired than the ornamented floors at the street level; but now, with a fuller understanding than German functionalism permitted, architects recognize that the building stated a total view of architecture: precise and mechanical in its shaft; decisive in its finish at the skyline; unbelievably satisfying in its ornamental base. Pedestrians respond without theorizing: the ornament suggests a movement that impels them to the protruding tower at the corner. A masterful stroke, that entrance tower is one of the finest transitions ever made at the corner of a building (plate 73). Its re-entrant angles clearly join the walls; its verticality anchors the horizontal bays that originate there. It is the emblem of the institution, a designator, and its theme is wholly harmonious, from its circular mullions to its bull's-eye windows and rampant foliate patterns.

Sullivan, pardonably, could not understand why his art did not win out over the legacy left by the Fair. He turned inward, marshalled his criticisms against society, and addressed an imaginary pupil to whom he passionately declared his exalted notions of brotherhood, of democracy, of altruism.

KINDERGARTEN CHATS, 1901–02

His dialogue is an epic; its dramatic organization unfolds in four scenes where nature is the setting. Sullivan first subjects his pupil to experiences that are literal and objective. The master offers philistine opinions, more or less cynical and brutal. One of Chicago's towers is ridiculed because it mocks the Lake, its "shifting color, its turbulence, its serenity, its smile and its frown."[45] A railroad terminal is nothing except confusion, " . . . holy in iniquity, where to go in you go out, and to go out you go in; where to go up you go down, and to go down you go up."[46] After he has criticized several examples of " . . . wretchedly tormented structure . . . ,"[47] the master inserts Taine's idea: each building is the image of the man who made it; the " . . . study of architecture . . . [is] a branch of social science. . . . "[48]

There follows a transition to the subjective, the refined, the altruistic. A peaceful scene, "The Oasis," leads the student to Richardson's Marshall Field Warehouse: "Let us pause, my son, at this Oasis. . . . " Still mindful of the earlier ridicule, we hear Sullivan say, "I mean that stone and mortar, here, spring into life, and are no more material and sordid things. . . . "[49] Then, this lesson, too, is generalized: All real values are subjective.

The student becomes impatient, demands facts, and asks for a discussion of ornament and proportion; but Sullivan declines: First, concentrate on essentials, and he warns against the fugacious and superficial nature of words. Principles of life must come first, insight especially into Function and Form: "That which exists in the spirit ever seeks and finds its physical counterpart in form, its visible image."[50] The master becomes expansive: "All is function, all is form, but the fragrance of them is rhythm, the language of them is rhythm. . . . "[51] The student whimpers, but the master is relentless: " . . . each part must so clearly express its function that the function can be read through the part . . . if the work is to be organic. . . . "[52]

Ultimately, the pupil is permitted to return to the world of fact, the "barbaric yawp that now fills the air."[53] A commemorative Doric column to be erected at Detroit causes the Master to ask what relation it bears to the primeval forest and the early settlers, and he concludes the first lessons with a plea for social expression: " . . . arrange your architecture for Democracy, not for Imperialism. . . . "[54]

Having become divested of his misconceptions, the student is confused; the Master seizes that moment to suggest a journey. "No more architecture for me; no more of the stuffy city,"[55] says the student. The master now substitutes the natural for the artificial, and, together, the men witness a violent thunderstorm in the first of four encounters with nature, "Summer." The storm inspires a duet as master and pupil rhyme the lightning, wind and rain. "Wildly, the Earth, in glutton frenzy, drinks it up: *Spilling at the mouth*—Rolling in flood, and racket. *And delirious, gray gloom!*" "Bravo!" shouts the Master in an exultant passage ending the scene, "You concluded bravely! Now why doesn't it occur to you to do that in your architecture?"[56]

The boy is left alone in the country, he reels pathetically in his ecstasy, and a butterfly poised like a fairy on a flower inspires him to write a mawkish poem: "They call you Psyche, dainty soul; I call you sweetheart, honey-seeker."[57] He has a crippling revelation: "To think that I could not make a poem to a butterfly!"[58]

His aborted flight into eloquence returns a humble, dejected student to the city, back to the objective, where once again he is undiscerning. Renewed attacks upon architectural follies and aberrations sharpen his senses. But he feels lost and inadequate, and when the master attacks Columbia University's Library as a Classical "dry and vacant seed-pod"[59] (plate 80), the student longs to return to his former learning. "I quit! Do you understand me? I quit! Let me go back. . . . "[60] He rants irrationally, attacks democracy (" . . . the crawling-in-place of the common, the average, the vulgar.")[61] and throws idealism away (" . . . the dollar is everything. . . . ").[62]

The master assuages the student by one of the most inspired passages in *Kindergarten Chats* where Democracy is said to be a moral principle, a spiritual law, intended for men who have the right of choice: " . . . a certain function, democracy, is seeking a certain form of expression, democratic architecture. . . . "[63] But one almost Kierkegaardian glimpse at New York shows that man, despite his powers to create, to inquire, to feel, to emote, to dream, to choose, has abused his power, and the City stands for selfishness gone mad, not organization but disorganization, and so does Chicago, " . . . this foul spot on the smiling prairie. . . . "[64] New York and Chicago are "miscarriages of democracy,"[65] where strong minds " . . . clash in the fierce rut of ambition."[66]

On that note, Sullivan shifts to a scene, "Autumn Glory," where the student surely proceeds to learn the elements of architecture; the pier, the lintel, the arch. Then the discussion arrives at a definition of architecture as the need and the power to build. But art cannot be different from its civilization, and the civilization cannot be different from education, so " . . . the first duty of our architectural educators must be to make of their pupils good citizens; and that . . . never can be accomplished so long as they continue to cram their confiding pupils full of trashy notions concerning the 'classic,' and utterly ignore their own land and people. . . . "[67]

A tragic sense overwhelms the master and the pupil as they recognize their idealism, and pessimism now brings "that winter which congeals all nobility of thought. . . . "[68] The master ridicules talk of composition, but speaks of organization as an evolution from within, and he is generally vague and uninformative, save for one observation, "Proportion is a result, not a cause."[69]

Mention of ornament buoys the master, again in his poetic realm of subjectivities, and the dialogue ends optimistically with a Spring song: "the volcanic warmth of life. . . . The glory and the gentleness of her power will come to you. Use it wisely; use it well."[70]

It was a pathetic appeal to the future, made by a disappointed man.

5. *A FRESHENING SPRING*

For Louis Sullivan himself there was no Spring. There continued to be many personal indignities: the loss of his property in Ocean Springs in 1908, the departure of draftsmen one by one, the auction of his art and furniture in 1909, withdrawal from the Chicago Club in 1910, his retreat to a wretched hotel in 1911, removal from his offices in the Auditorium Tower in 1918, and the cessation of commissions after 1919, except for one small façade he made for a music shop in Chicago in 1921.

But his Socratic *Kindergarten Chats* inspired young architects, who kept alive the "ardor of his hope in a new architecture." Despite the Gothic Woolworth Tower that Gilbert erected in New York, despite the Classic Lincoln Memorial that Henry Bacon built at Washington, Sullivan saw hopeful signs, particularly in the work of former apprentices like Purcell and Elmslie and, above all, Wright, whose friendship now returned so that both together rejoiced in Wright's successes at Buffalo, Chicago and Tokyo.

Sullivan saw that he was not society's only victim; in 1923 he wrote an incensed criticism of the award made by the *Chicago Tribune* Competition's jury, who had failed to judge that Eliel Saarinen's design was superior to the Gothic tower which brought Raymond Hood the first prize. But, for all his complaints against Hood's false buttresses and Gothic pinnacles, Sullivan's criticism had lost its sting; having released skyscrapers from the inhibiting philosophy of structural realism, Sullivan had unwittingly provided a rationale for treating form independently of its structure. A Sullivan might do so by creating an original, expressive symbol that did not violate the structure, but dexterous formalists like Hood too frequently seized the opportunity to apply any mantle, first Gothic and, just as easily, something modern when streamlining became more eye-catching for his clients.

Lacking commissions from that clientele, Sullivan spent much time reading, notably in Whitman's *Leaves of Grass,* and some young architects persuaded him to write his autobiography in 1922–23 and to design nineteen plates of ornament, which were published in 1924, the year of his death (plates 81–84).

His occasional buildings, infrequent as they were, continued to be vital, individual and masterful, but his architecture bore a pensive humility, and, in touching upon less exalted problems than the skyscraper, it became more lyric and incidental in its themes.

Considered superficially, some of Sullivan's final designs reveal the inspiration he received from Wright. The Babson Residence, for instance, which Sullivan built at Riverside, Illinois, in 1907 (plate 78) is generally reminiscent of Wright's Coonley House in the same town. More than any other building by Sullivan, the Babson house is a sequence of accents articulated along a horizontal axis, and it is closely united with its lawns, trees, gardens and service buildings. Salient porches and a *porte-cochère* magnify the deep punctures made for voids. But even this exercise in boldly-struck horizontalities remained a matter of substantial masses rather than the planes, trellises and walls that shape Wright's hollow volumes.

Again Sullivan went his own way, and never better than in a series of small banks for country towns in the mid-West, beginning with the one at Owatonna, Minnesota, which is the best of all. The National Farmers' Bank, erected in 1907–08, has a wonderful geometry both in its mass and, significantly, in its interior space also. Its plan is a square with cashiers' counter at one end; apparently, that arrangement was determined early by the bank's officers. One of them, Carl K. Bennett, read an article Sullivan had written for *The Craftsman* in 1906, and he asked its author to suggest how to obtain something better than the usual Roman bank.

His answer was a brick block, nearly a cube, shot through by two arched spaces (plates 85, 86). But the touch of a master appears in what Sullivan did with that theme. Take the organization of the elevations: a base of reddish-brown sandstone ashlar supports large walls of rough shale brick, variegated in their rough texture and soft dark-red colors; two arched windows, spanning a colossal thirty-six feet, stand beneath wide archivolts made by ten concentric header courses, and the glass is set in slender steel mullions; those basic masses and voids are capped by a broad cornice, again made in brick and unique in design, though one might have expected that no imagination could have created still another consistent but varied pattern.

The composition does not end there; an enormous hierarchy of scale brings a surround for the walls, consisting of bronze-green frames, in which bouquets of leaves and brown acorns decorate an inner band of brilliant glass mosaic, which glistens with specks of green, white and gold. Still closer, we see plaques in the upper corners, where geometric figures are interlaced with luxuriant scrolls and leaves (plate 90). Thus Sullivan had outgrown the criticism Root made of his early work, for the Bank has that organization which is possessed, and only rarely, by the greatest examples of architecture: it strikes its geometric silhouette from afar and consistently unfolds its theme until the closest inspection still reveals consonant shapes, textures, colors, and ornament.

Owatonna's Bank offers three further lessons. It is surely Sullivan's most successful interior space, for its geometry and subdivisions and lighting all consistently reinforce the statement made by the mass. Moreover, if our attention can turn to the furnishings for a moment, the paintings, furniture and especially the clock and tellers' wickets show Sullivan's insistence upon making utilitarian things become more than mere unrelated tools (plates 91–97); he neither exposed the machine, nor hid it; rather he adorned it and made it sculptural—a mature understanding that satisfying performance does not occur if naked machines are permitted to intrude their severe lines into the human world.

But Owatonna offers one more note, only a suggested one, unfortunately. A portion of the Bank's lot was reserved for a two-story wing that contains stores, offices and a small warehouse. Together, the bank and the office building indicate how Sullivan might have treated a whole town. The two buildings share a common base, but in its upper story, the office wing begins a new but compatible statement in its band of arched windows, which creates an individual variation within the unified façade (plates 87–88). Admittedly, there is no suggestion about urban spaces; nor are we told how monumental buildings might be set apart; but the hint is tantalizing, and America is the loser for not having called for Sullivan's talent.

After the supreme achievement at Owatonna, Sullivan's buildings, it seems to me at least, show a falling-off in some respects. Ornament tended to become an adornment placed over simple structural patterns, but not quite related to them. A department store for the Van Allen Company impresses me as being somewhat dismembered. It was built at Clinton, Iowa, in 1913–15, and although it is a small building, it employs skeletal construction so that large plate-glass windows afford abundant light. Its mullions and spandrels soberly state the rectilinear grid of the frame, which might have no grace at all were it not that Sullivan allowed one façade to burst its mullions into exuberant foliage at their summits (plate 100). The strong stalks are vigorous, but they seem more purely ornamental than the integral ornament Sullivan made at Owatonna.

Besides, the later buildings couple the decorative with an increasing interest in large plain surfaces, sometimes treated so as to fracture the geometry into unrelated planes. That tendency is apparent at Grinnell, Iowa, where Sullivan's Merchants' National Bank, built in 1914, is essentially a single cubic mass that presents two elevations (plate 101). Each is different in its organization, rhythms, fenestration and ornament so that, presented separately, one might not have guessed that they belong to one building. The dissonances are dominated by the continuous cornice and the massive, shale-brick walls, which still do not subdue the heavy ornament above the door. Yet, Sullivan's bank—except for Walter Burley Griffin's house and the new library that Skidmore, Owings & Merrill designed for Grinnell College—is the only building (among streets loaded with false fronts, Gothic pinnacles and Moorish phantasies) that rivals the magnificence which autumn maples bring to Grinnell. One who has seen it, therefore, tends to regard the fractured mass and incompatibilities with the charitable affection readily given to those whose irregularities endear them.

A more successful handling of ornamented planes attached to a cubic mass stands at Sidney, Ohio, where Sullivan built the People's Savings & Loan Association Bank in 1917–18. He is said to have considered this the best of the series. It does offer rich combinations of fine materials, notably verde antique marble and gilded bronze, and it is scrupulously complete in the architect's command over total environment, right down to the blue glass mosaics in its tympanum, the foliage in its corbels, and its robust furniture. But its large pattern of rectilinear fenestration overpowers the west elevation, which, unfortunately, remains unrelated to the panel above the entrance (plates 104–106).

Indeed, such strong forms and rhythms came off best when Sullivan worked with masses, and his last bank, that at Columbus, Wisconsin, built in 1919, shows his talent well. The entire building is severely rectilinear, and while the interior space is subdivided disappointingly (by partitions that oppose the axes of the dominant geometry and light), the slightly battered lateral wall contains an ornamented arcade and deep buttresses in a strong composition that declares one fact: that architecture, as an art, must be a rhythmic cadence of solids and voids which will receive sunlight gloriously (plates 107–111).

Because of that revelation, Sullivan shall never lack luster. To insist, as I have, upon his early vision of an elm tree and a suspension bridge—which are sculptural or structural but not spatial images—to have marked his commonplaces before

1890, to have stressed his arrival through classicism, his theory for an organic style, and his command of traditional principles of composition, should suggest that his genius made architecture grow by evolution from the past, not from fitful and doctrinaire manifestoes associated with ephemeral and journalized revolutions. That he did not achieve an architecture of fine spaces, that he made no predictions for the city, that he was not an innovator in engineering should not obscure his message.

For Sullivan taught that the language of modern society is both science and romance, both fact and belief, and that the two must be wedded in one statement. He broadened the technology of his own day by making it poetic, and he brought it as a symbol to serve the institutions of industrial society; his art arose from his organization of the scientific ideas, technical means, utilitarian demands, and romantic beliefs of his age.

No one realized Sullivan's meaning better than Thorstein Veblen, whose *The Higher Learning in America* adopted Sullivan's philosophy of architecture as a basis for criticizing the extravagant and wasteful irrelevancies in the Gothic buildings erected for the University of Chicago. Sullivan properly belongs in that Chicago group of intellectuals, including Veblen and John Dewey, who founded their revolt against classical idealism in a new pragatism.[71] But the pragmatism was mature, for it never insisted, as many who came late to the industrial machine, including Walter Gropius, naïvely insisted, that utilitarian expedience and economy should be declared in bald and mechanistic displays of raw technology.[72]

One might have thought that Sullivan's poetic transformation of the machine might prevent any further Gothic spire from rising on America's hills, any further factory from blackening her valleys. But that was not so; and when, occasionally, better planning occurred, it was more likely to be done by the Burnhams and not by the Sullivans.

There are Burnhams among us now, as Philadelphians see in their artless wonder, the new Penn Center; as Bostonians will shortly see in Back Bay's coming Prudential Center; in neither case does technology serve man well. The question is whether there are Sullivans we are neglecting.

The Notes to the Text begin on page 114.

1. Frank Furness, Pennsylvania Academy of Fine Arts, Philadelphia, 1872.

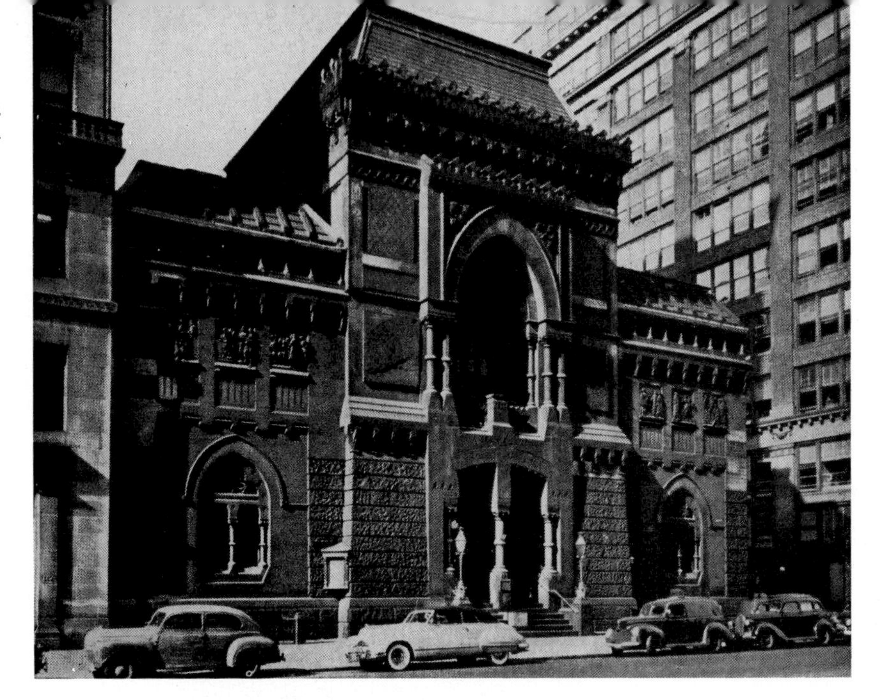

2. Ward Pavilion, Johns Hopkins University Hospital, Baltimore, Maryland, 1888 (above).

3. Ware & Van Brunt, Memorial Hall, Harvard University, Cambridge, Massachusetts, 1875.

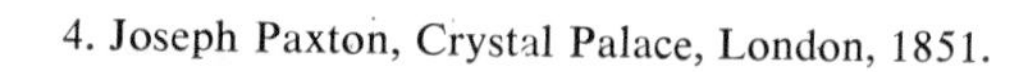

4. Joseph Paxton, Crystal Palace, London, 1851.

5. Viollet-le-Duc, "Iron and Masonry—Vaulting of Large Spaces," from *Discourses on Architecture,* 1889.

6. H. H. Richardson, American Express Building, Chicago, 1872.

7. Three Houses for Dankmar Adler, Dila Kohn and Eli Felsenthal, Chicago, 1885-86.

8. Borden Block, Chicago, 1879-80.

9. Rothschild Store, Chicago, 1880-81.

10. Revell Building, Chicago, 1881-83.

11. Ryerson Building, Chicago, 1884.

12. Troesher Building, Chicago, 1884.

14. Auditorium. Preliminary design.

15. Auditorium. Preliminary design.

13. Selz, Schwab & Co., Factory, Chicago, 1886-87 (opposite page).

16. Auditorium Building, Chicago, 1886-90. Exterior (opposite page).

17. Auditorium. Interior.

18 Auditorium. Organ grille and boxes.

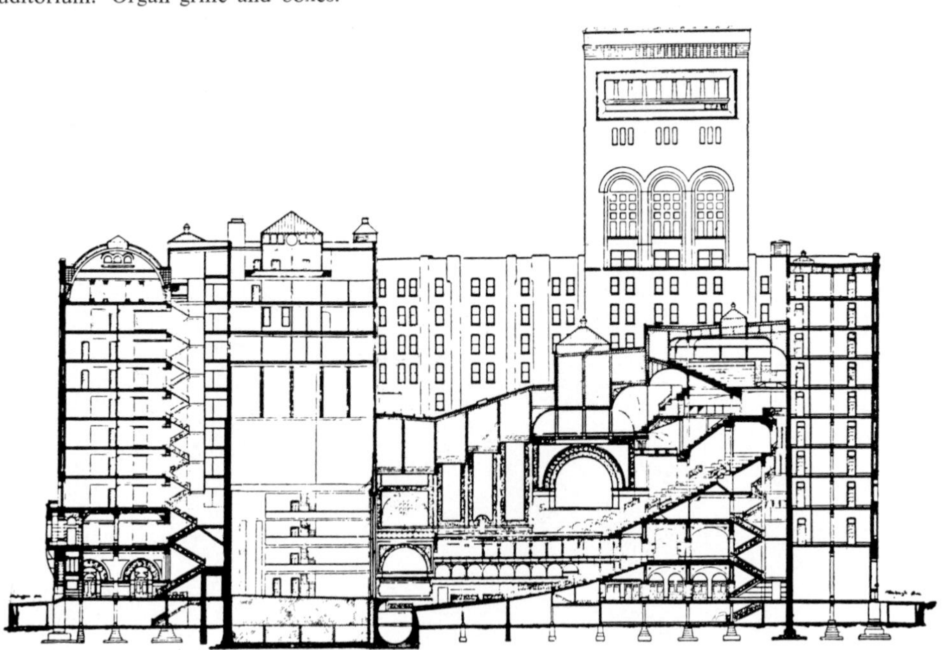

19. Auditorium. Section.

20. Auditorium. Stairs.

21. Auditorium. Bar.

22. H. H. Richardson, Marshal Field Wholesale Warehouse, Chicago, 1885-87.

23. Dooly Block, Salt Lake City, 1890-91.

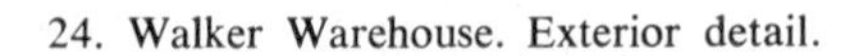

24. Walker Warehouse. Exterior detail.

25. Walker Warehouse, Chicago, 1888-89.

26. Walker Warehouse. Exterior detail.

27. Burnham & Root, Reliance Building, Chicago, 1890-95.

28. Cold Storage Exchange Warehouse, 1891.

29. Getty Tomb, Graceland Cemetery, Chicago, 1890.

30. Getty Tomb. Bronze gate.

31. Getty Tomb. Inner door.

32. Getty Tomb. Side view.

33. Anshe Ma'ariv Synagogue, Chicago, 1890-91.

34. Anshe Ma'ariv Synagogue. Preliminary design.

35. Anshe Ma'ariv Synagogue. Interior.

36. Ryerson Tomb, Graceland Cemetery, Chicago, 1889.

38. Vacation Cottage, Ocean Springs, Mississippi, 1890.

39. Louis Sullivan at Ocean Springs.

37. Louis Sullivan and his wife at Ocean Springs (opposite page).

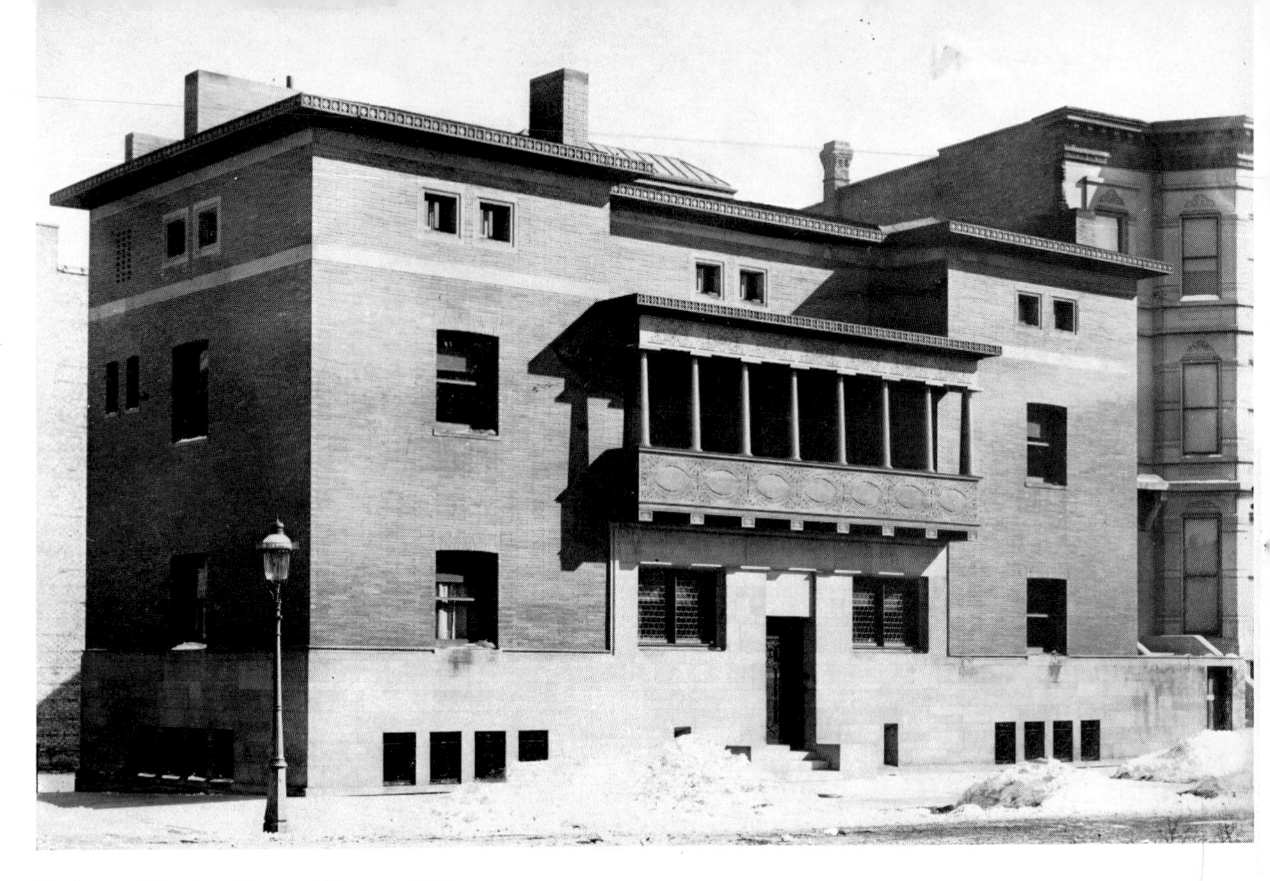

40. James Charnley House, Chicago, 1892.

41. Albert W. Sullivan House, Chicago, 1892.

42. Wainwright Tomb, Bellefontaine Cemetery, St. Louis, 1892.

43. Transportation Building, Chicago, 1890-91. "Golden Door."

44. Transportation Building.

45. Wainwright Building, St. Louis, 1890-91.

46. Wainwright Building.
Side view.

48. Wainwright Building. Façade detail.

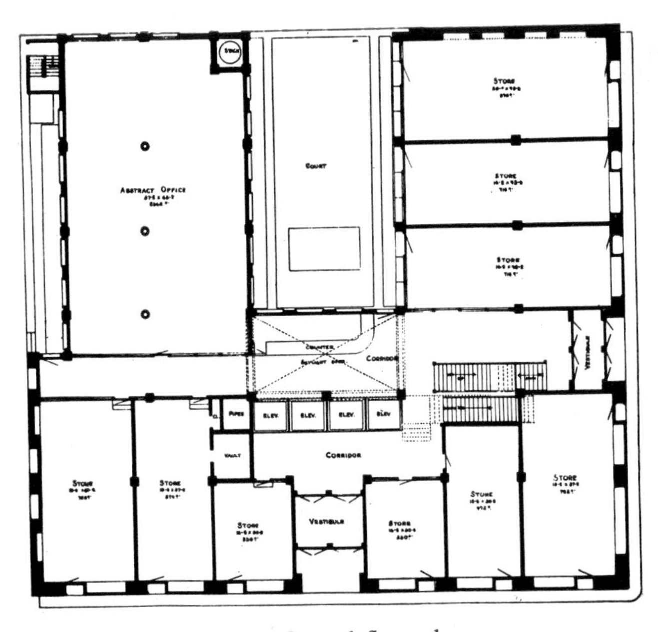

49. Wainwright Building. Ground floor plan.

47. Wainwright Building. Exterior view (opposite page).

50. Schiller Building, Chicago, 1891-92.

51. Design for Fraternity Temple, 1891 (opposite page).

FRATERNITY TEMPLE ASSOCIATION.
I.O.O.F.
Adler and Sullivan
Architects

52. Stock Exchange Building, Chicago, 1893-94.

53. Stock Exchange Building. Exterior detail.

54. Guaranty Building, Buffalo, 1894-95.

55. Guaranty Building. Façade.

56. Guaranty Building. Façade.

GUARANTY
GUARANTY

58. Guaranty Building. Ground floor.

. Guaranty Building. Main entrance (opposite page).

59. Guaranty Building. Capital detail.

60. Guaranty Building. Side entrance.

61. Guaranty Building. Foyer.

62. Guaranty Building. Elevator cage.

53. Guaranty Building. Foyer detail.

64. Guaranty Building. Stair.

65. Gage Building, Chicago, 1898-99. (With four additional stories.) (opposite page).

66. Gage Building. Side view.

67. Gage Building. Original façade.

68. Bayard Building, New York, 1897-98.

69. Bayard Building. Façade detail.

70. Bayard Building. Façade detail under cornices.

71. Bayard Building. Entrance.

72. Carson Pirie Scott Store (formerly Schlesinger & Mayer Department Store) Chicago, 1899-40.

73. Carson Pirie Scott Store. (With cornice alteration.)

74. Carson Pirie Scott Store.
Upper façade detail.

75. Carson Pirie Scott Store.
Lower façade detail.

76. Carson Pirie Scott Store. Entrance pavilion.

77. Carson Pirie Scott Store. Detail of ornament, entrance pavilion (opposite page).

78. Henry Babson House, Riverside, Illinois, 1907.

79. D. H. Burnham & Co., Fuller Building, New York, 1902.

80. McKim, Mead & White, Low Library, New York, 1895-97.

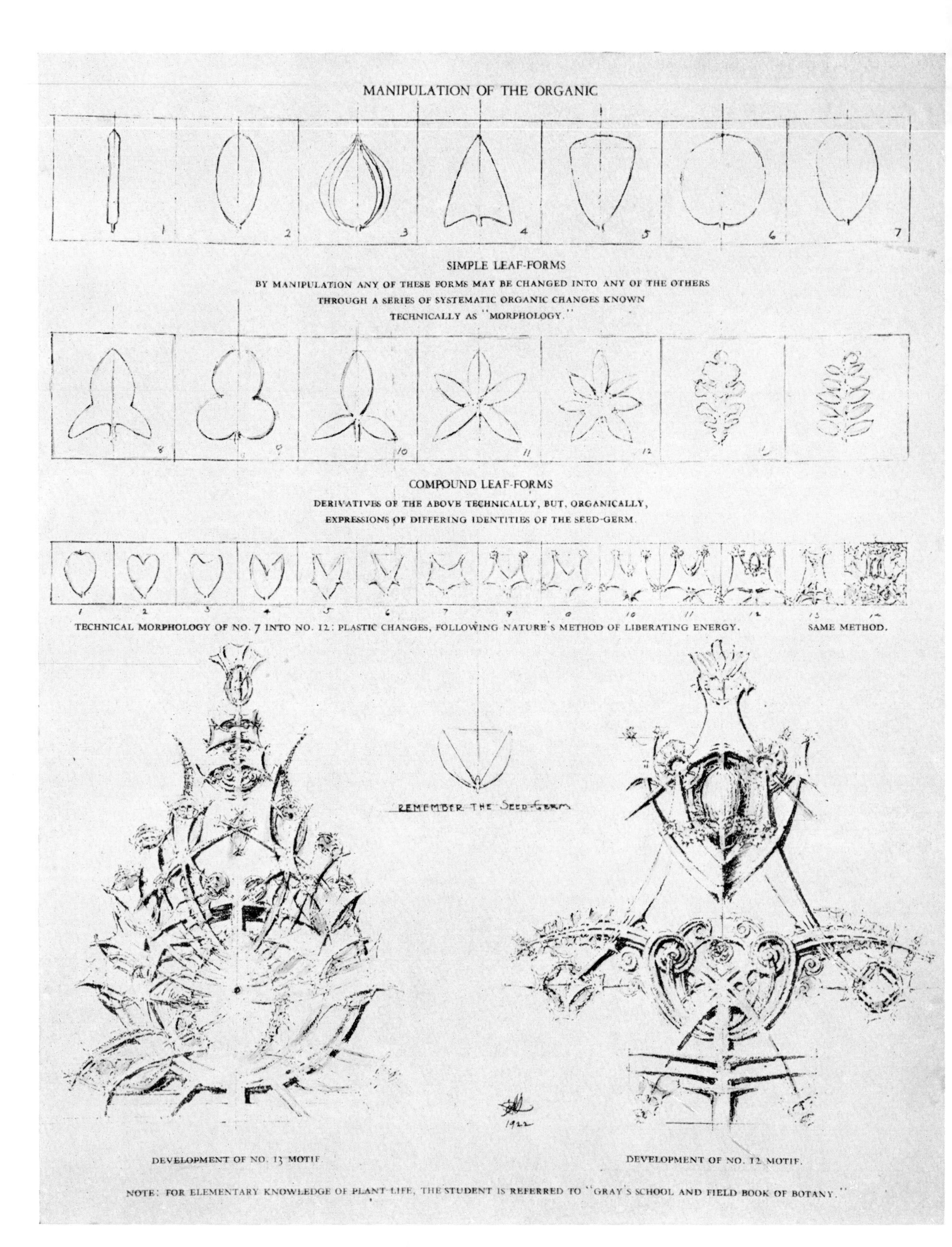

81. Plate 2 from Louis Sullivan, *A System of Architectural Ornament According with a Philosophy of Man's Powers,* 1924.

82. Plate 11 from *A System of Architectural Ornament* (opposite pa

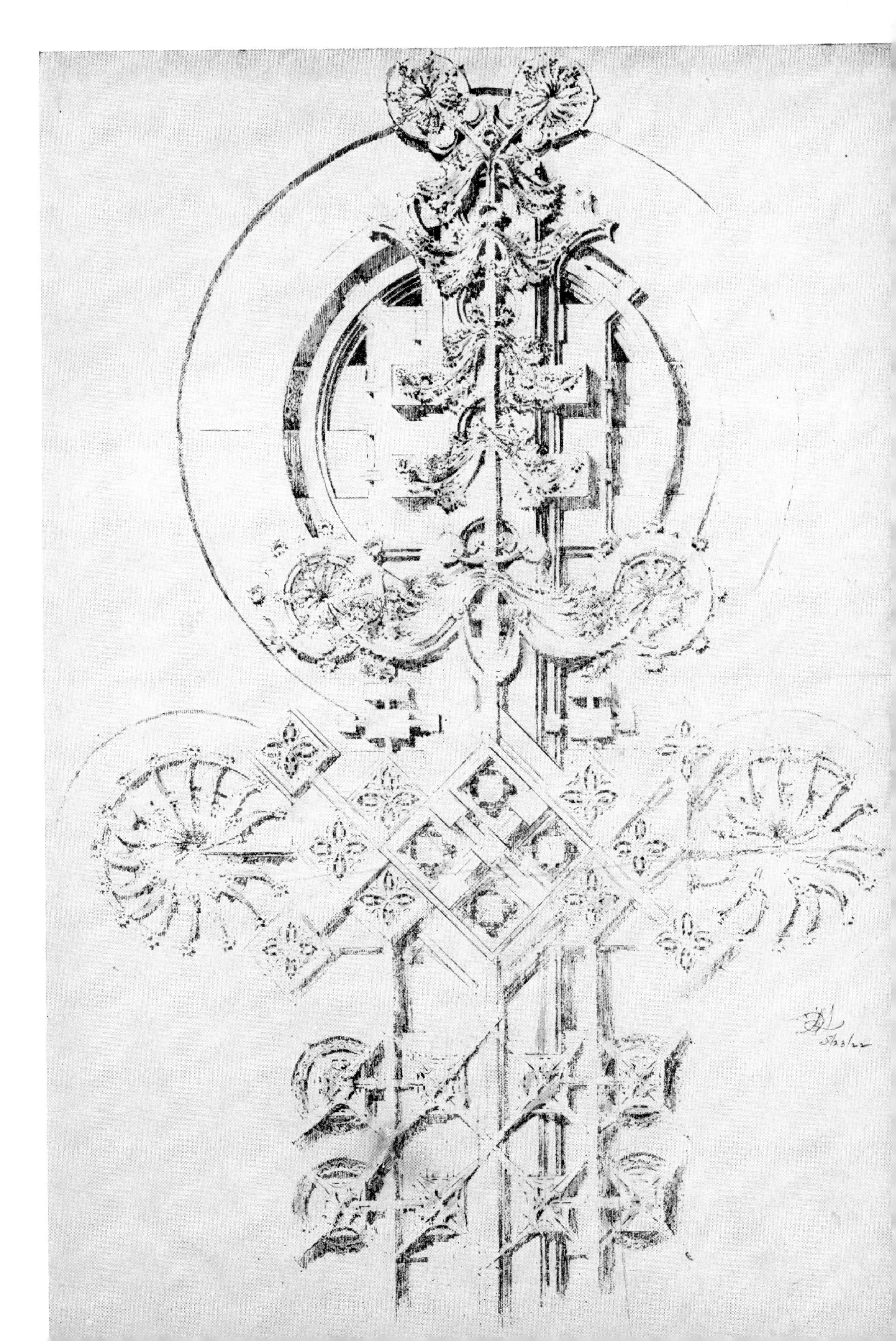
5/23/22

83. Plate 14 from *A System of Architectural Ornament.*

84. Plate 16 from *A System of Architectural Ornament* (opposite page).

IMPROMPTU

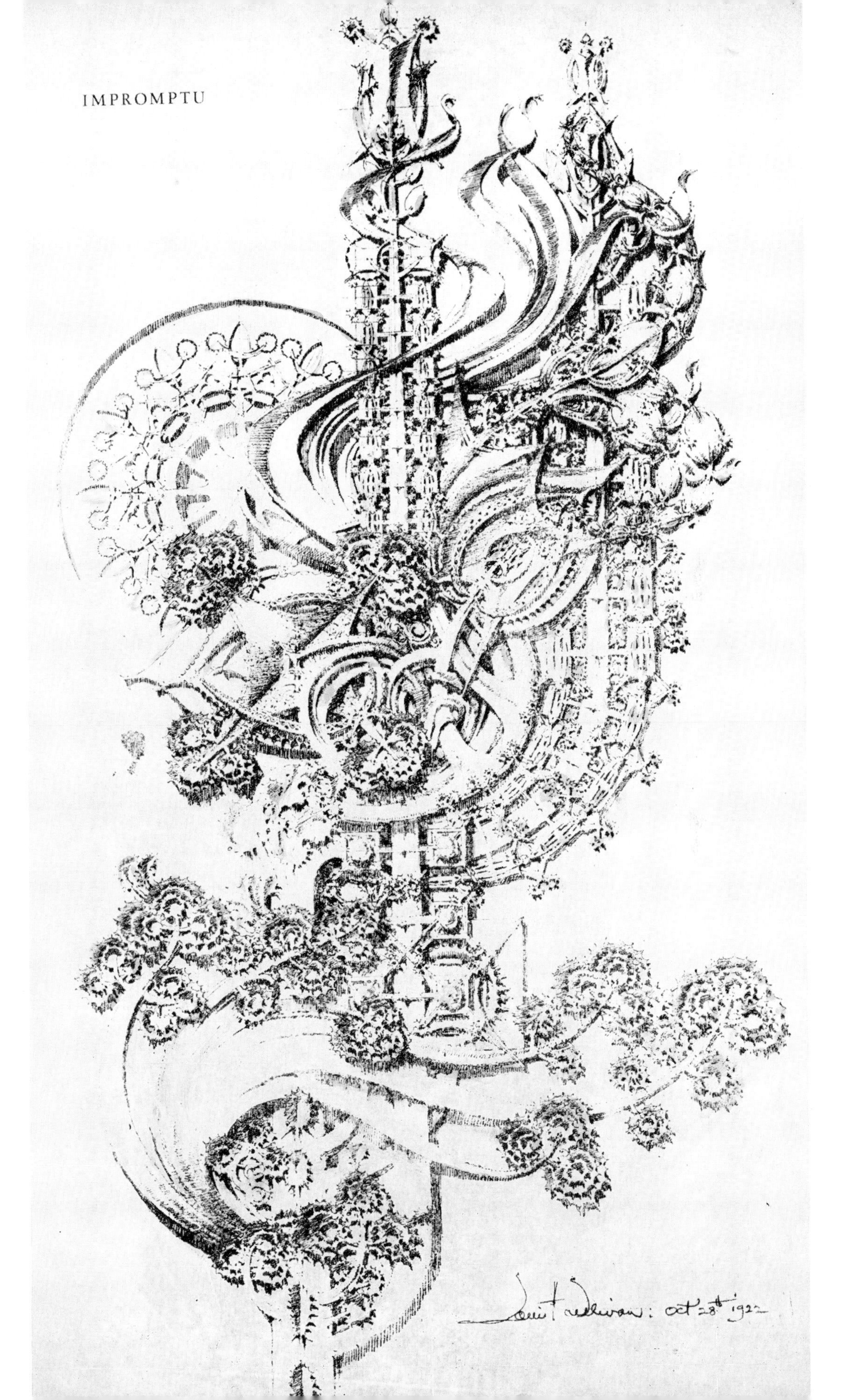

85. National Farmers' Bank, Owatonna, Minnesota, 1907-08.

86. National Farmers' Bank, Owatonna.

87. National Farmers' Bank, Owatonna. Side view showing rear offices.

88. National Farmers' Bank, Owatonna.

89. National Farmers' Bank, Owatonna. Exterior detail.

90. National Farmers' Bank, Owatonna. Terra cotta mold for iron ornament. (Photo on opposite page shows casting in place.)

91. National Farmers' Bank, Owatonna. Interior toward entrance (opposite page).

92. National Farmers' Bank, Owatonna. Interior entrance detail.

3. National Farmers' Bank, Owatonna. Interior (opposite page).

94. National Farmers' Bank, Owatonna. Interior detail.

95. National Farmers' Bank, Owatonna. Interior detail.

96. National Farmers' Bank, Owatonna. Interior toward teller's wicket.

97. National Farmers' Bank, Owatonna. Teller's wicket (opposite page)

98. Home Building Association Bank, Newark, Ohio, 1914.

99. Home Building Bank, Newark. Side façade.

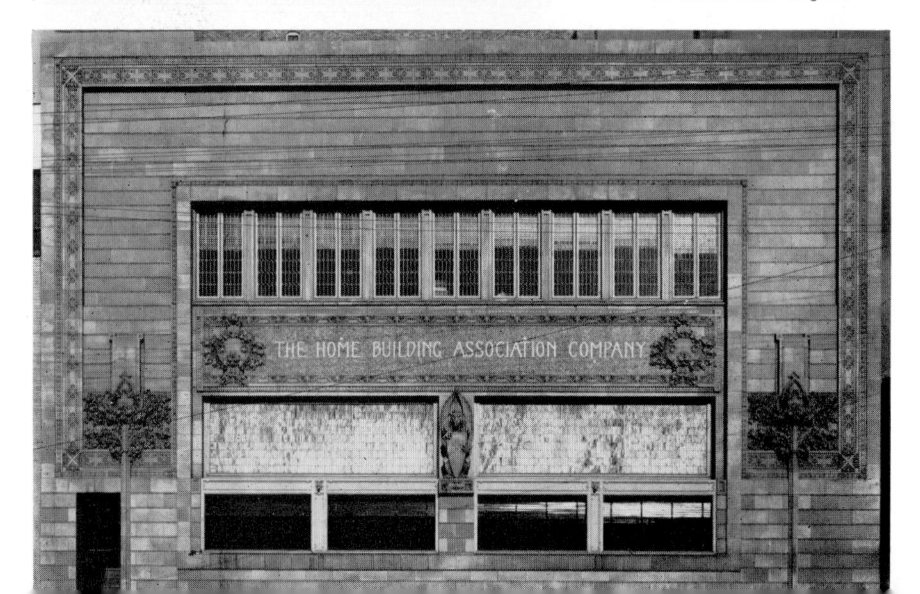

100. Van Allen Store, Clinton, Iowa, 1913-15.

101. Merchants' National Bank, Grinnell, Iowa, 1914.

102. Merchants' National Bank, Grinnell. Interior.

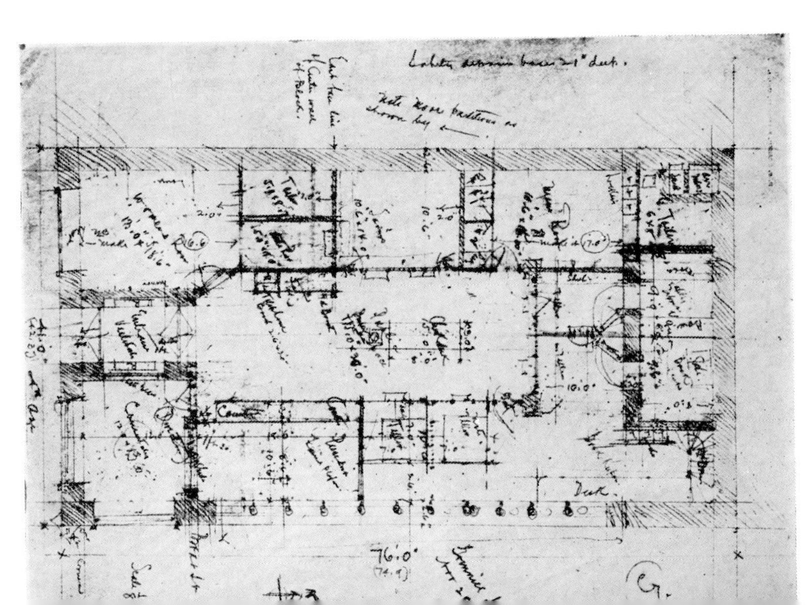

103. Merchants' National Bank, Grinnell. Plan.

104. Peoples' Savings and Loan Association Bank, Sidney, Ohio, 1917-18.

105. Peoples' Savings Bank, Sidney. Interior.

106. Peoples' Savings Bank, Sidney. Interior office detail.

FARMERS & MERCHANTS
UNION BANK
1861
1919
SULLIVAN ARCHITECT
FARMERS & MERCHANTS UNION BANK

107. Farmers' and Merchant's Union Bank, Columbus, Wisconsin, 1919 (opposite page).

108. Farmers' Union Bank, Columbus. Side view.

109. Farmers' Union Bank, Columbus. Side façade detail.

110. Farmers' Union Bank, Columbus. Exterior.

111. Farmers' Union Bank, Columbus. Interior.

K

NOTES

1. Sullivan, *The Autobiography of an Idea,* Dover Publications, Inc., New York, 1956, pp. 234 ff.
2. Sullivan, *Kindergarten Chats on Architecture, Education and Democracy,* Scarab Fraternity Press, Washington, D.C., 1934, p. 47.
3. *Autobiography,* p. 64.
4. *Ibid.,* p. 290.
5. *Ibid.,* p. 290.
6. Sullivan, in "The Tall Office Building Artistically Considered," *Lippincott's Magazine,* March, 1896; reprinted, *Kindergarten Chats and Other Writings,* Wittenborn, New York, 1947, p. 203.
7. *Ibid.,* p. 205.
8. *Ibid.*
9. *Ibid.,* p. 206.
10. *Ibid.*
11. *Autobiography,* p. 117.
12. *Ibid.,* p. 188.
13. *Ibid.,* p. 200.
14. Sullivan, Letter to his Brother, Albert, December 6, 1874, quoted, Willard Connely, "New Sullivan Letters," *Journal of the American Institute of Architects,* July, 1953, pp. 9 ff.
15. Claude Bragdon, quoted, Willard Connely, "New Chapters in the Life of Louis Sullivan," *Journal of the American Institute of Architects,* Sept., 1953, pp. 107 ff.
16. Thomas Huxley, speech at Johns Hopkins, quoted Albert Bush-Brown, "Get an Honest Brick-layer! The Scientists' Answer to Ruskin," *Journal of Aesthetics and Art Criticism,* Mar., 1958, pp. 348 ff.
17. See Albert Bush-Brown, "This New Shell Game: Function, Structure, Symbolism —or Art," *Architectural Record,* June, 1957, pp. 185 ff.
18. *Kindergarten Chats,* p. 117. For an extensive discussion of the situation Sullivan described, see John E. Burchard and Albert Bush-Brown, *Architecture in America, A Social Interpretation,* Boston, Atlantic–Little Brown [1961], Chapters II and III.
19. V. B., "Archaeology and the Vernacular Architecture," *The American Architect and Building News,* Apr., 1878, p. 143.
20. See Willard Connely, *JAIA,* Sept., 1953, pp. 108 ff.
21. *Kindergarten Chats,* p. 45.
22. John Wellborn Root, quoted, *Louis Sullivan and the Architecture of Free Enterprise,* ed., Edgar Kaufmann, Jr., The Art Institute of Chicago, 1956, p. 32.
23. Henry Van Brunt, "Architecture in the West," *Atlantic Monthly,* LXIV, 1889, p. 778.

THE GERM: THE SEAT OF POWER

Above is drawn a diagram of a typical seed with two cotyledons. The cotyledons are specialized rudimentary leaves containing a supply of nourishment sufficient for the initial stage of the development of the germ.

The Germ is the real thing; the seat of identity. Within its delicate mechanism lies the will to power: the function which is to seek and eventually to find its full expression in form.

The seat of power and the will to live constitute the simple working idea upon which all that follows is based—as to efflorescence.[73]

112. Krause Music Store, Chicago, 1922 (opposite page).

24. Anonymous critic, "The Fagin Building," *Architectural Record,* II, 1892–93, p. 472.
25. César Daly, "La Semaine des Constructeurs," transl., W. A. Otis, *Inland Architect and News Record,* XV, 6, 1890, p. 5.
26. Gottfried Semper, "Development of Architectural Style," transl., J. W. Root, *Inland Architect and News Record,* XIV, 7, 1889, p. 76.
27. *Ibid.,* pp. 76 f. For a discussion of the theory of style and composition that underlies my interpretation of Sullivan's architecture, see Albert Bush-Brown, with Imre Halasz, "Notes Toward a Basis for Criticism," *Architectural Record,* Oct., 1959, pp. 183 ff.
28. Frederick Baumann, "Discussion," *Inland Architect and News Report,* Sept., 3, 1887, p. 26.
29. Sullivan, "Style," *Inland Architect and News Record,* Nov. 6, 1888, pp. 59 f.
30. S. T. Coleridge, *Lectures on Shakespeare and Other Poets and Dramatists,* E. P. Dutton and Co., N. Y., 1909, p. 46.
31. *Autobiography,* p. 258.
32. *Ibid.,* pp. 254 f.
33. *Ibid.*
34. *Kindergarten Chats,* p. 158.
35. Donald D. Egbert, "The Idea of Organic Expression and American Architecture," *Evolutionary Thought in America,* ed., Stow Persons, Yale University Press, New Haven, 1950, pp. 336 ff. Also see Albert Bush-Brown, "The Architectural Polemic," *Journal of Aesthetics and Art Criticism,* XVIII, 2, 1959, pp. 143 ff.
36. Sigfried Giedion, *Space, Time and Architecture,* Harvard University Press, Cambridge, 1949, p. 324. The point of view also appears in Hugh Morrison, *Louis Sullivan,* Museum of Modern Art, N. Y., 1935, p. 63; see also Henry R. Hope, "Louis Sullivan's Architectural Ornament," *Magazine of Art,* March, 1947, pp. 111 ff.
37. Sullivan, "What is the Just Subordination, in Architectural Design, of Details to Mass?" *Inland Architect and News Record,* April, 1887, reprinted, *Kindergarten Chats and Other Writings,* Wittenborn, New York, 1947, p. 185.
38. *Kindergarten Chats,* p. 149.
39. Grant Manson, "Sullivan and Wright, an Uneasy Union of Celts," *Architectural Review,* Nov., 1955, pp. 297 ff.
40. *Autobiography,* p. 313.
41. Daniel Burnham, quoted, Hugh Morrison, *Sullivan,* p. 182.
42. Daniel Burnham, quoted, Charles Moore, *Daniel Burnham, Architect and Planner,* Houghton Mifflin, Boston, II, p. 166.
43. *Autobiography,* p. 322.
44. *Ibid.,* p. 325.
45. *Kindergarten Chats,* p. 1.
46. *Ibid.,* p. 6.
47. *Ibid.,* p. 9.
48. *Ibid.,* p. 8.
49. *Ibid.,* p. 15.
50. *Ibid.,* p. 39.
51. *Ibid.,* p. 41.
52. *Ibid.,* p. 43.

53. *Ibid.*, p. 50.
54. *Ibid.*, p. 83.
55. *Ibid.*, p. 93.
56. *Ibid.*, pp. 96 ff.
57. *Ibid.*, p. 103.
58. *Ibid.*, p. 107.
59. *Ibid.*, p. 111.
60. *Ibid.*, p. 118.
61. *Ibid.*, p. 119.
62. *Ibid.*
63. *Ibid.*, p. 127.
64. *Ibid.*, p. 142.
65. *Ibid.*, p. 152.
66. *Ibid.*, p. 148.
67. *Ibid.*, p. 169.
68. *Ibid.*, p. 214.
69. *Ibid.*, p. 232.
70. *Ibid.*, pp. 255 f.
71. Morton G. White, *Social Thought in America, The Revolt against Formalism,* The Viking Press, N. Y., 1949.
72. Lewis Mumford, "Frank Lloyd Wright and the New Pioneers," *Architectural Record,* LXV, 1929, p. 414, where he suggests the interesting idea: ". . . Mr. Wright is not the forerunner of Le Corbusier but, in a real sense, his successor."
73. Sullivan, quoted, Louis Sullivan, *A System of Architectural Ornament According with a Philosophy of Man's Powers,* Press of the American Institute of Architects, Washington, 1924; from his introduction to the nineteen plates of architectural ornament contained in the book.

SELECTED CHRONOLOGICAL LIST OF BUILDINGS AND PROJECTS

ADLER AND SULLIVAN

1879–80	Borden Block, N.W. corner of Randolph and Dearborn Streets, Chicago
1881	Rothschild Store, 210 W. Monroe Street, Chicago
1881–83	Revell Building, N.E. corner Wabash and Adams Streets, Chicago
1884	Ryerson Building, 16-20 East Randolph Street, Chicago
1885–86	Adler Residence, 3542 Ellis Avenue, Chicago
1886–87	Selz, Schwab & Co. Factory, N.E. corner of Superior and Roberts Streets, Chicago
1886–90	Auditorium Building, Michigan Avenue and Congress Street, Chicago
1888–89	Walker Warehouse, 200-214 South Market Street, Chicago
1889	Ryerson Tomb, Graceland Cemetery, Chicago
1890	Sullivan Cottage, Ocean Springs, Mississippi Getty Tomb, Graceland Cemetery, Chicago Falkenau Residence, 3420-24 Wabash Avenue, Chicago
1890–91	Dooly Block, 111 West 2nd Street South, Salt Lake City
1890–91	Wainwright Building, N.W. corner of 7th and Chestnut Streets, St. Louis
1890–91	Kehilath Anshe Ma'ariv Synagogue, S.E. corner 33rd and Indiana, Chicago (*now* Pilgrim Baptist Church)
1891	Fraternity Temple Design (*not executed*) Cold Storage Exchange Warehouse
1891–92	Schiller Building, 64 West Randolph Street, Chicago
1892	Charnley Residence, 1365 Astor Street, Chicago Albert W. Sullivan Residence, 4575 Lake Park Avenue, Chicago

1892 Wainwright Tomb, Bellefontaine Cemetery, St. Louis

1893–94 Transportation Building, World's Columbian Exposition, Chicago

1894–95 Guaranty Building, S.W. corner of Church and Pearl Streets, Buffalo (*now* Prudential Building)

LOUIS SULLIVAN

1897–98 Bayard Building, 65-69 Bleeker Street, New York (*now* Condict Building)

1898–99 Gage Building, 18 South Michigan Avenue, Chicago

1899–04 Schlesinger & Mayer Department Store, S.E. corner of Madison and State Streets, Chicago (*now* Carson Pirie Scott Department Store)

1907–08 National Farmer's Bank, N.E. corner of Broadway and Cedar Streets, Owatonna, Minnesota (*now* Security Bank)

1907 Babson Residence, 230 Riverside Drive, Riverside, Illinois

1911 People's Savings Bank, corner of 3rd Avenue S.W. and 1st Street S.W., Cedar Rapids, Iowa

1913–15 J. D. Van Allen and Co. Dry-Goods Store, N.W. corner of 5th Avenue and South 2nd Street, Clinton, Iowa

1914 Merchant's National Bank, N.W. corner of 4th Avenue and Broad Street, Grinnell, Iowa

1917–18 People's Savings and Loan Association Bank, S.E. corner of Court Street and Ohio Avenue, Sidney, Ohio

1919 Farmer's and Merchant's Union Bank, N.W. corner of James Street and Broadway, Columbus, Wisconsin

CHRONOLOGY

1856	Born Louis Henri Sullivan, September 3, Boston
1872	Entered Massachusetts Institute of Technology (left at end of first year)
1873	Draftsman, office of Furness & Hewitt, Philadelphia
1874	Entered Ecole des Beaux Arts, Paris (left after short period)
1875–79	Draftsman in Chicago for various firms
1879	Joined office of Dankmar Adler, Chicago
1881	Became full partner in the architectural firm of Adler & Sullivan
1895	Partnership with Adler dissolved, Sullivan continues alone
1899	Married Margaret Hattabough (divorced in 1917)
1901–02	Sullivan wrote the series of "Kindergarten Chats" for the *Interstate Architect and Builder*
1922–23	"The Autobiography of an Idea" appeared serially in the *Journal of the American Institute of Architects* while Sullivan worked concurrently on the drawings for *A System of Architectural Ornament According with a Philosophy of Man's Powers*
1924	Died in Chicago
1946	Posthumous award of the Gold Medal of the American Institute of Architects

SELECTED BIBLIOGRAPHY OF BOOKS AND ARTICLES WRITTEN BY LOUIS SULLIVAN

A System of Architectural Ornament According with a Philosophy of Man's Powers, Press of the American Institute of Architects, Washington, 1924. (Nineteen drawings with notes, made by Sullivan during 1922-23.) The original drawings are in the Burnham Library, Art Institute, Chicago.

"Concerning the Imperial Hotel, Tokyo," *Architectural Record,* April, 1923, pp. 333-352.

Democracy: A Man Search. (Unpublished work completed in 1908. In Avery Architectural Library, Columbia University, N. Y., and Burnham Library, Art Institute, Chicago; Micro-card publication in 1949 by the Louisville Free Public Library, Kentucky.)

"Development of Construction," *The Economist,* June 24, 1916, p. 1252; July 1, 1916, pp. 39-40.

"Emotional Architecture as Compared With Classical, a Study in Objective and Subjective," *Inland Architect & News Record,* November, 1894, pp. 32-34.

Inspiration, Inland Architect Press, Chicago, 1886.

Kindergarten Chats and Other Writings, Wittenborn, N. Y., 1947. (This includes several of Sullivan's most important articles and addresses to architectural groups, some of which are here listed individually.)

"Natural Thinking: A Study in Democracy." (Talk given in 1905, unpublished. In Burnham Library, Art Institute, Chicago.)

"Ornament in Architecture," *Engineering Magazine,* August, 1892, pp. 633-644.

"Reflections on the Tokyo Disaster," *Architectural Record,* February, 1924, pp. 113-117.

The Autobiography of an Idea, Dover Publications, New York, 1956. (W. W. Norton, N. Y., 1934; Peter Smith, N. Y., 1949; originally appeared as a series in the *Journal of the American Institute of Architects,* June, 1922–August, 1923.)

"The Chicago Tribune Competition," *Architectural Record,* February, 1923, pp. 151-157.

"The Tall Office Building Artistically Considered," *Lippincott's,* March, 1896, pp. 403-409.

"The Young Man in Architecture," *The Brickbuilder,* June, 1900, pp. 115-119.

"What is Architecture? A Study in the American People of Today," *American Contractor,* January 6, 1906, pp. 48-54.

"What is the Just Subordination, in Architectural Design, of Details to Mass?" *Inland Architect & News Record,* April, 1887, pp. 51-54.

"Wherefore the Poet?" *Poetry,* March, 1916, pp. 305-307.

SELECTED BIBLIOGRAPHY ON LOUIS SULLIVAN

in Bragdon, Claude, *Architecture and Democracy,* Knopf, N. Y., 1926.

Bragdon, Claude, "Letters from Louis Sullivan," *Architecture,* July, 1931, pp. 7-10.

Connely, Willard, *Louis Sullivan As He Lived,* Horizon Press, N. Y., 1960.

Connely, Willard, series of Sullivan articles, *American Institute of Architects Journal,* July, 1953; September, 1953; November, 1953; December, 1953; May, 1954; October, 1954; December, 1954; January, 1955.

in Egbert, Donald D., "The Idea of Organic Expression and American Architecture," *Evolutionary Thought in America,* ed., Stow Persons, Yale University Press, New Haven, 1950.

Ferree, Barr, "The High Building and Its Art," *Scribner's,* March, 1894, pp. 297-318.

in Giedion, Sigfried, *Space, Time and Architecture,* (3rd ed.) Harvard University Press, Cambridge, 1954.

in Hitchcock, Henry-Russell, *The Architecture of H. H. Richardson,* Museum of Modern Art, N. Y., 1936.

Hitchcock, Henry-Russell, "Sullivan and the Skyscraper," *Journal of the Royal Institute of British Architects,* July, 1953, pp. 353-361.

Hope, Henry R., "Louis Sullivan's Architectural Ornament," *Magazine of Art,* March, 1947, pp. 111-117.

Kaufmann, Edgar, Jr., ed., *Louis Sullivan and the Architecture of Free Enterprise,* The Art Institute, Chicago, 1956 (catalog and commentary on Sullivan exhibition).

Kimball, S. Fiske, "Louis Sullivan, an Old Master," *Architectural Record,* April, 1925, pp. 289-304.

"Louis H. Sullivan—His Work," *Architectural Record,* July, 1924, pp. 28-32.

"Louis Sullivan, the First American Architect," *Current Literature,* June, 1912, pp. 703-707.

Manson, Grant, "Sullivan and Wright, an Uneasy Union of Celts," *Architectural Review,* November, 1955, pp. 297-300.

Morrison, Hugh, *Louis Sullivan, Prophet of Modern Architecture,* Museum of Modern Art and W. W. Norton, N. Y., 1935; reprinted, with additions, Peter Smith, New York, 1952 (bibliography extended to 1951).

Morrison, Hugh, "Louis Sullivan Today," *Journal of the American Institute of Architecture,* September, 1956.

in Mumford, Lewis, *The Brown Decades,* a study of the Arts in America, 1865-95, (2nd ed.) Dover Publications, N.Y., 1955.

in Pevsner, Nikolaus, *Pioneers of Modern Design from William Morris to Walter Gropius,* (2nd ed.) Museum of Modern Art, N. Y., 1949.

Rebori, A. N., "An Architecture of Democracy," *Architectural Record,* May, 1916, pp. 437-465.

Robertson, Howard, "The Work of Louis H. Sullivan," *Architect's Journal,* June 18, 1924, pp. 1000-1009.

Schuyler, Montgomery, "A Critique of the Works of Adler & Sullivan," Great American Architects Series, #2, published separately by *Architectural Record,* December, 1895.

Schuyler, Montgomery, *Studies in American Architecture,* Harper & Bros., New York, 1892.

"The 'Skyscraper' Up to Date," *Architectural Record,* January-March, 1899, pp. 231-257.

White, Morton G., *Social Thought in America, The Revolt against Formalism,* The Viking Press, New York, 1949.

in Wright, Frank Lloyd, *An Autobiography,* Longmans Green, N. Y., 1932.

in Wright, Frank Lloyd, *Genius and the Mobocracy,* Duell, Sloan & Pearce, N. Y., 1949.

Wright, Frank Lloyd, "Louis Sullivan, Beloved Master," *Western Architect,* June, 1924, pp. 64-66.

INDEX

Numbers in regular roman type refer to text pages; *italic* figures refer to the plates.

SOURCES OF ILLUSTRATIONS

Architectural Record, Oct., 1908: 88; July, 1915: 79
Architectural Review, Nov., 1951: 1
Courtesy Art Institute, Chicago, Illinois: 11, 12, 18, 24, 25, 26, 31, 90, 92
Chicago Architectural Photographing Company (Henry Fuermann), Chicago, Illinois: 16, 17, 20, 27, 29, 30, 32, 35, 37, 38, 39, 40, 41, 43, 44, 50, 52, 54, 57, 58, 60, 61, 62, 63, 64, 65, 66, 67, 76, 78, 87, 89, 96, 97, 98, 99, 101, 102, 103, 104, 105, 106, 108, 109, 110, 111
Chicago Historical Society, Chicago, Illinois: 8, 10
Courtesy Columbia University News Service, New York: 80
Ewing Galloway, New York: 4
Harper's Weekly, Sept. 8, 1888: 2
Courtesy Harvard University News Service, Cambridge, Massachusetts: 3
Hedrich-Blessing, Chicago, Illinois: 45, 46, 48, 73, 74
Infinity Inc., Minneapolis, Minnesota: 85, 86, 91, 93, 94, 95
Inland Architect & News Record, July, 1888: 19; Oct., 1890: 28
Journal of the Society of Architectural Historians, March/May, 1950: 6
Victor Laredo, New York: 69, 70, 71
Courtesy Museum of Modern Art, New York: 13, 14, 15, 21, 22, 23, 33, 34, 36, 42, 49, 51, 68, 72, 100, 112
Hugh Morrison, *Louis Sullivan,* Peter Smith, New York, 1952: 7, 9
Louis Sullivan, *A System of Architectural Ornament According with a Philosophy of Man's Powers,* Press of the American Institute of Architects (Washington, 1924): 81, 82, 83, 84
From *The Idea of Louis Sullivan* by John Szarkowski. Copyright © 1956 by the University of Minnesota. Published by the University of Minnesota Press: 47, 53, 55, 56, 59, 75, 77, 107
Viollet-le-Duc, from *Discourses on Architecture* II, Lecture XII, Grove Press Edition (New York, 1959): 5